Teachers as Readers

Perspectives on the Importance of Reading in Teachers' Classrooms and Lives

Michelle Commeyras
Betty Shockley Bisplinghoff
Jennifer Olson
University of Georgia
Athens, Georgia, USA
EDITORS

INTERNATIONAL
Reading Association
800 Barksdale Road, PO Box 8139
Newark, Delaware 19714-8139, USA
www.reading.org

The International Reading Association attempts, through its publications, to provide a forum for a wide spectrum of opinions on reading. This policy permits divergent viewpoints without implying the endorsement of the Association.

Director of Publications   Joan M. Irwin
Editorial Director, Books and Special Projects   Matthew W. Baker
Production Editor   Shannon Benner
Permissions Editor   Janet S. Parrack
Acquisitions and Communications Coordinator   Corinne M. Mooney
Associate Editor, Books and Special Projects   Sara J. Murphy
Assistant Editor   Charlene M. Nichols
Administrative Assistant   Michele Jester
Senior Editorial Assistant   Tyanna L. Collins
Production Department Manager   Iona Sauscermen
Supervisor, Electronic Publishing   Anette Schütz
Senior Electronic Publishing Specialist   Cheryl J. Strum
Electronic Publishing Specialist   R. Lynn Harrison
Proofreader   Elizabeth C. Hunt

Project Editor   Sara J. Murphy

Cover Design   Linda Steere

Library of Congress Cataloging-in-Publication Data
Teachers as readers : perspectives on the importance of reading in teachers' classrooms and lives / Michelle Commeyras, Betty Shockley Bisplinghoff, Jennifer Olson, editors.
   p. cm.
Includes bibliographical references.
 ISBN 0-87207-006-9
1. Reading teachers–Books and reading–United States–Case studies.
2. Reading–United States–Language experience approach–Case studies.
I. Commeyras, Michelle. II. Bisplinghoff, Betty Shockley. III. Olson, Jennifer.
IV. International Reading Association.
 LB2844.1.R4 T43 2003
 428'.4--dc21
                        2003001202

CONTENTS

Debbie Barrett
W.R. Coile Middle School
Athens, Georgia, USA

Betty Shockley Bisplinghoff
University of Georgia
Athens, Georgia, USA

Sarah Bridges
Fowler Drive Elementary
Athens, Georgia, USA

Tricia Bridges
Washington Wilkes Primary
   School
Washington, Georgia, USA

Aimee Castleman
West Jackson Primary School
Winder, Georgia, USA

Michelle Commeyras
University of Georgia
Athens, Georgia, USA

Sharon Dowling Cox
Honey Creek Elementary School
Conyers, Georgia, USA

Margret Echols
Dearing Elementary School
Dearing, Georgia, USA

Vicki Gina Hanson
Maysville Elementary School
Maysville, Georgia, USA

Marybeth Harris
Oglethorpe County Elementary
   School
Lexington, Georgia, USA

Jill Hermann-Wilmarth
University of Georgia
Athens, Georgia, USA

Betty Hubbard
University of Georgia
Athens, Georgia, USA

Jennifer Olson
University of Georgia
Athens, Georgia, USA

Barbara Robbins
Edwards Middle School
Conyers, Georgia, USA

Annette Santana
University of Georgia
Athens, Georgia, USA

Dawn Spruill
Walker Park Elementary School
Monroe, Georgia, USA

Renèe Tootle
Maysville Elementary School
Maysville, Georgia, USA

Lori Whatley
Dearing Elementary School
Dearing, Georgia, USA

Maxine Greene, whom we admire for her philosophical wisdom on education, wrote, "If it weren't for Jo March in *Little Women*, I wouldn't be where I am today" (Greene, 1995, p. 91). Imagine Greene saying that to a classroom of students. Imagine you had not read Louisa May Alcott's *Little Women* (1869/1997). Would you want Greene to tell you about Jo March? Would you want her to explain how one book, *Little Women*, and one character, Jo March, could have a profound effect on her life? Can you imagine that after Greene told you more about her reading of this book that you might choose to read it yourself (motivation)? As a reader you might learn about how a more experienced reader thinks about the text as it relates to his or her life (text-to-life and life-to-text connections). You might hear that Greene has reread *Little Women* throughout her life and why she did so (reading to learn and remember). Greene might read you selections from the book to explain how she has made sense of the story (comprehension and interpretation) or to talk about how some turn of phrase Alcott wrote was poignant, poetic, or prosodic (author's craft). Greene might speculate about a word and its connotations in 1869 when Alcott published the book (vocabulary). We can only imagine what students might have learned about reading from hearing Greene talk about Jo March and *Little Women*.

Creating a Seminar for Teachers as Readers

To inform and recruit graduate students for a seminar titled Readers as Teachers and Teachers as Readers, Michelle Commeyras, a member of the Department of Reading Education faculty at the University of Georgia, circulated the following one-page announcement:

> This graduate seminar is for teachers interested in having reading lives apart from their teaching lives. It is for teachers committed to attending more fully and expansively to their

personal reading lives. And it is for those of us curious to know more explicitly and specifically how one's personal reading life might be brought to bear on one's teaching life. For example, as I attend more to how I find and choose what to read, I can use that self-knowledge in teaching my students to be more self-directed in their reading lives. Just imagine what more a group of teachers might learn together in an inquiry-based seminar that pursues the question, What is the potential of a teacher's personal reading for enhancing teaching in general and specifically teaching reading and language arts? It will be important that seminar participants currently be teaching in settings from prekindergarten to university students.

The International Reading Association's position statement *Excellent Reading Teachers* (2000) makes no mention of the teacher being a reader—having a reading life beyond that of reading to students and being familiar with children's literature. It seems that educators have overlooked the potential significance of the teacher as reader. Ask most any literacy teacher educator about the reading habits and interests of those preparing to be teachers. Most likely, you will hear that many do not like to read, have lost their love of reading, or rarely find time to read. In my undergraduate teacher education courses, I have begun addressing this in discussions with students. A former student gave the following response to explain her reluctance to read:

> I believe that my dislike for reading was based upon my childhood experience with reading, in that I struggled with reading as well as spelling. Much of my interaction with literature and texts was negative and was done only when required by teachers or professors. [This semester] I have grown as a reader in the sense that I am excited about reading, and I am choosing to read more voluntarily. In reference to what kind of reader I want to be, I believe my interest in reading will continue to grow and be nurtured through a wide variety of text sources. (A preservice teacher in her junior year)

In offering a graduate seminar on the reader as teacher and teacher as reader, I seek to continue my own reading life alongside inservice teachers wanting time to engage in meaningful ways with reading in their everyday lives. This seminar provides time and space for each participant to set personal reading goals and to select readings to meet those goals. Each participant will be engaged in a self-study of themselves as readers and themselves as readers who teach. Ultimately, we will document what we have learned about being teachers that read and readers that teach.

Soon after distribution of the announcement, Michelle heard from teachers who were excited to take a course like this that would count toward their graduate degrees (Master of Education, Specialist in Education, Doctor of Education, and Doctor of Philosophy). She was not surprised. She already knew some teachers who wanted an opportunity to focus on themselves as readers. In a prior graduate course, Michelle had told teachers about the reading odysseys she and her undergraduate students did in a course Michelle regularly teaches (Commeyras, 2001). The Reading Odyssey assignment is intended to promote a culture of reading among those preparing to be teachers of reading. The assignment requires finding a variety of texts to read (whole books, chapters, essays, plays, poems, etc.) across at least eight subject categories (sciences; social sciences; philosophy; education; international and global issues; Asian, African, or Central/South American countries, cultures, or peoples; Native American, African American, or Hispanic American peoples; and gender issues). The teachers pursuing graduate studies asked, "Why can't we have a graduate course like that?"

Why not, indeed! Michelle pursued the possibility with her faculty colleagues, keeping in mind that the circumstances would be different. Teachers in graduate school who would register for Michelle's Readers as Teachers and Teachers as Readers seminar would most likely already be committed readers. The purpose would not be to develop a culture of reading among them; instead, it would be to find the significances of being readers to being teachers of reading and vice versa. The seminar would provide time and space for each participant to set personal reading goals and to select readings to meet those goals. Each participant would be engaged in a study of himself or herself as a reader who teaches.

Participating in the Seminar

Music was playing when teachers entered the university classroom every Tuesday afternoon for Readers as Teachers and Teachers as Readers (see Appendix on page 176 for seminar syllabus). It might be jazz. It might be classical. It might be African. It might be oldies. Whatever it was, it was intended to be welcoming and to create a thoughtful mood while we 18 educators, the course facilitators and participants, wrote on the whiteboard favorite quotations from what we had read that week (see Figure below). We also wrote titles and authors of readings that we thought important to share with others.

Figure. Example of quotations written on whiteboard by seminar participants.

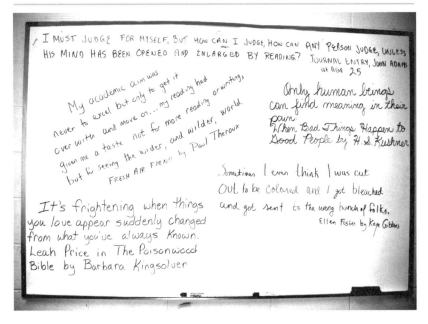

We were coming together to explore and name the relations between being readers and teachers. We were all women who came from a variety of teaching situations in prekindergartens, elementary schools, middle schools, and universities. Michelle's friend and faculty colleague, Betty Shockley Bisplinghoff, volunteered to help facilitate the seminar because of her own interests and research in the role of personal reading in teaching (Bisplinghoff, 2002a, 2002b).

Our weekly seminar sessions included any combination of the following activities:

- Discussions about the quotes, titles, and authors we wrote on the whiteboard
- Read-alouds from our books, magazines, newspapers, etc.
- Discussions about what happened when we shared ourselves as readers with our students
- Writing about what we were learning in terms of the potential of a teacher's personal reading for enhancing teaching in general and teaching reading and language arts specifically

Together, we documented what we had learned. After the first meeting, everyone agreed to have all seminar discussions tape-recorded as a shared resource because, from the beginning of the course, Michelle had talked about the possibility of collectively writing a book for other teachers of reading and language arts.

Creating a Book for Teachers as Readers

We all agreed to write essays in response to the seminar's umbrella question, What is the potential of a teacher's personal reading for enhancing teaching in general and teaching reading and language arts specifically? Betty organized the seminar participants into writing groups and advised us on how to support and advise one another in writing first and subsequent essay drafts. Eventually, everyone's essay was ready to be read to the entire group. For several weeks the seminar focused on listening to essays by three or four teachers during each session. Following each reading, the other teachers offered comments on what they found most engaging and what they thought needed more attention or development. Even after the seminar ended, everyone continued revising the essays as the possibility of making a book became increasingly real. Jennifer Olson, one of the seminar participants, accepted Michelle and Betty's invitation to join them as an editor on the book project. At the end of the seminar, Jennifer became particularly interested in the process of looking across the essays for what we now call teacher as reader stances. Her willingness to continue learning from what everyone had written, combined with her writing acumen, led Michelle and Betty to want her to join them as editors. Our combined efforts culminated in this book comprising 18 essays. For our readers' information, each author has prefaced her essay with a short biographical sketch.

We decided for our final session to think about significant connections between our collective experience and the standards provided by the International Reading Association in its 2000 position statement *Excellent Reading Teachers*. What could we add to these standards based on our new sensitivity and awareness that being readers ourselves could inform the way we taught reading and language arts? How might our ideas inform the emphasis on standards for excellent teachers of reading? Everyone wrote ideas on the whiteboard. The discussion we had became the inspiration for this book's final essay, "All Together Now: Proposing Stances for Teachers as Readers." We have drawn insights from all the essays to be explicit about what stances we have realized are possible when we never forget ourselves as readers when we teach reading.

Although there are a few books about teachers as readers, we have found none that explicitly focus on examining how the reading-teaching relationship might be heightened. Mary Kay Rummel and Elizabeth P. Quintero's 1997 book analyzes 13 teachers' reading histories with regard to their sensitivities to diversity. Wendy Atwell-Vasey's 1998 book chronicles her study of three teachers' reading experiences in relation to their teaching practices. In both books, researchers are analyzing and writing about other teachers.

There is a need for more information from teachers about the role of personal reading in their teaching lives. Many resources already exist about writers as teachers and teachers as writers. Apparently, it has been more self-evident that teaching the writing process is more authentic and informed when the teacher has personally experienced process writing (Keffer et al., 1996). Accomplished writers have written about the relationship between being a writer and teaching writing (Baumbach, 1970). There is even a nonprofit organization, Teachers & Writers Collaborative, that is dedicated to the idea that writers should make a unique contribution to the teaching of writing. Would it be odd for there to be a parallel organization called Teachers & Readers Collaborative, dedicated to the idea that readers should make a unique contribution to the teaching of reading? Writing expertise in the form of poems, articles, and books is tangible, whereas reading expertise seems indiscernible. Obviously there are more of us who see ourselves as expert readers than expert writers, but even the reading experts with doctoral degrees rarely invoke their own reading lives when researching and recommending reading instruction. The textbooks on methods of teaching reading do not mention using our adult reading to teach reading to children.

This book is for all those teachers who want to be readers *and* teachers. Our hope is that this book will inspire you to explore ways of bringing your reading self to teaching reading and language arts. And, we want to further encourage those who already share their reading life with students. Join us in reading to learn and reading to lead!

REFERENCES

Atwell-Vasey, W. (1998). *Nourishing words: Bridging private reading and public teaching*. Albany, NY: State University of New York Press.

Baumbach, J. (Ed.). (1970). *Writers as teachers: Teachers as writers*. Austin, TX: Holt, Rinehart and Winston.

Bisplinghoff, B.S. (2002a). Teacher planning as responsible resistance. *Language Arts, 80*, 119–128.

Bisplinghoff, B.S. (2002b). Under the wings of writers: A teacher reads to find her way. *The Reading Teacher, 56*, 242–252.

Commeyras, M. (2001). Pondering the ubiquity of reading: What can we learn? *Journal of Adolescent & Adult Literacy, 44*, 520–524.

Greene, M. (1995). *Releasing the imagination: Essays on education, the arts, and social change*. San Francisco: Jossey-Bass.

International Reading Association. (2000). *Excellent reading teachers*. A position statement of the International Reading Association. Newark, DE: Author.

Keffer, A., Carr, S., Lanier, B., Mattison, L., Wood, D., & Stanulis, R. (1996). Teacher researchers discover magic in forming an adult writing workshop. *Language Arts, 73*, 113–121.

Rummel, M.K., & Quintero, E.P. (1997). *Teachers' reading/Teachers' lives*. Albany, NY: State University of New York Press.

LITERATURE CITED

Alcott, L.M. (1997). *Little women*. New York: Puffin. (Original work published 1869)

—Michelle Commeyras—
TEACHER EDUCATOR

Michelle has taught undergraduate and graduate students in the University of Georgia's Department of Reading Education since 1991. Her previous teaching experiences include teacher assistant in a preschool for children with special emotional needs and disruptive behaviors, teacher assistant in a junior high school classroom for students considered behaviorally disturbed, visiting teacher leading critical reading discussions with elementary school children identified as gifted, teacher of U.S. history at a private secondary school, museum educator at the John F. Kennedy Library, sixth-grade teacher in a public school, teacher of life skills to adults considered profoundly mentally retarded, and Visiting Fulbright lecturer on gender issues at the University of Botswana in southern Africa.

A favorite reading of Michelle's during the Readers as Teachers and Teachers as Readers seminar was Katherine Frank's biography of Mary Kingsley. Michelle gets vicarious pleasure from reading about women travelers and explorers, particularly those who have gone to Africa. Kingsley was a woman of Victorian England who traveled in west Africa with black Africans as her guides and companions.

CHAPTER 1

We Laughed Often: We Readers as Teachers
Michelle Commeyras

or 15 weeks we met. We were 19 women readers who teach. We were 19 teachers who read. And we laughed often as we explored how our personal reading mattered to our teaching and how our teaching lives mattered to our reading lives. I remember laughing somewhat self-consciously when Barbara Robbins, a reading and language arts teacher of academically gifted seventh- and eighth-grade students, talked about reading *Crazy in Alabama* (Childress, 1993), a book her mother had recommended. Barbara warned us that it was "crazy and demented."

She told us that the narrator's aunt kills her husband and chops off his head with an electric kitchen knife. This is before the aunt heads for Hollywood, California, where she's going to be on the television show *Beverly Hillbillies*. I think we were laughing in horror when Barbara explained, "She's heading for Hollywood, and she's got Chester's head in a hatbox. She can't find a respectful way to get rid of it, so she keeps going along with it."

Barbara then observed, "And it makes no sense. There's this dichotomy. She poisoned her husband; then, when she thought he was not really dead, she decapitated him. Then she whipped out his head in front of her Mama when her Mama didn't believe that she killed him."

Lori Whatley, who teaches first grade, got a big laugh from us when she said, "I know those people in that book. They live in Thomsen, Georgia." She, too, had read *Crazy in Alabama*. Barbara told us that she had told her students that very day about an episode she had just read in *Crazy in Alabama*. She was using the episode to make a point about one of the vocabulary words they were studying—*antiseptic*. Just imagine how intrigued her seventh-grade students were when she told them that while the narrator is cutting grass for an older lady, he is hit in the eye with a rock. His eye falls out on his cheek. In shock he runs to tell the old lady what has happened, and when she sees him, she keels over dead. Barbara explained that it was not antiseptic for his eyeball to be out of its socket.

Barbara said that her seventh-grade boys were very keen to know the title of the book, but she did not tell. She figured if they knew the title, they would go get the book and the outrageous content would surely lead to some flack from parents.

Betty Shockley Bisplinghoff, assistant professor in the Department of Elementary Education at the University of Georgia and cofacilitator of the seminar, was intrigued with the idea of cultivating mystery in presenting oneself as reader to students. Extending the idea, Betty B. imagined the first day of school with the teacher saying, "You know, I have been with a book before that scared me so badly that I had a hard time walking into a bookstore." She saw the potential of this kind of drama in setting up seventh graders to want to be readers.

Our conversations that evening and thereafter blended sharing what we were reading with one another, what we were doing to share our reading selves with our students, and further imagining the possibilities for connecting ourselves as readers with ourselves as teachers. Our point of departure was the observation that in the International Reading Association's position statement *Excellent Reading Teachers* (2000), no mention is made of the teacher being a reader, that is, having a reading life beyond that of reading to students and being familiar with children's literature. We seminar participants shared the goal of discovering the potential significance of the teacher as reader.

> We seminar participants shared the goal of discovering the potential significance of the teacher as reader.

We may have laughed often and thoroughly enjoyed laughing, but there was no doubt that we were serious about reading and teaching. In just three hours that evening early in our journey, we covered many topics that added new possibilities to what one could do as a teacher of reading that was not commonly thought of as part of reading instruction. How would these understandings matter for our teaching and our students?

Do I Want to Finish?

We also had an extended discussion about beginning to read something and then deciding we did not want to finish it. Renèe Tootle, a prekindergarten teacher, told us about selecting a Mitford Series book (Karon & Nelson, 1999) to read because she wanted to broaden her horizons because she mostly reads romance novels. She said, "I just don't know if I can get into it, but I tried real hard."

That prompted me to ask, "What does it mean when you say 'I tried real hard'?"

Renèe's response led her to speculate that perhaps she tried reading the book in the wrong context. She teaches prekindergarten children, and she had initiated a kind of sustained silent reading time during which she would read while the children looked at books. She found that she often was distracted from her own reading because she was so interested in watching what the children were doing with the books.

Sharon Dowling Cox, a speech-language pathologist for elementary students, talked about having waited for our seminar to read Terry MacMillan's *A Day Late and a Dollar Short* (2001), and how, much to her surprise now, it did not feel like the right time to read this kind of story. She realized that she was not in the mood for reading about other people's problems. She confessed, "I put it down. And that's the first time I've done that in a long time."

With my mind continually searching for links between our reading lives and our teaching lives, I asked if anyone ever stopped reading a book to their students before it was finished. Jill Hermann-Wilmarth had. She once tried reading *The Giver* (Lowry, 1993) to her fifth-grade students, but after the second chapter she put it away. The students told her they did not like it, so they found a different book to read aloud.

Margret Echols, a prekindergarten teacher, told us that she was having difficulty continuing with the book *When Bad Things Happen to Good People* (Kushner, 1981) because it was challenging some of her beliefs and that made her uncomfortable. She had told

Lori, while driving to class together, that she probably was not going to finish the book. With the demands of beginning a new school year, she did not feel willing to take on yet one more challenge. Three weeks later, we learned that Margret had returned to this book after the terrorist attacks on the United States on September 11, 2001. The world had changed, and Margret's needs as a reader changed, too.

In talking about books that we decided not to finish, we realized that this was a good example of something a teacher could share about her reading life with her students. How often do we as teachers talk with our students about beginning a book and then deciding not to finish it? How often do we tell them about the reasons why we decided to abandon the book? How often do we tell them about a book we once abandoned but later returned to? We realized that this was not something that we typically thought of as teaching reading and that this was not included in any state or national standards for reading. However, now it seemed an important aspect of reading to address as teachers.

> How often do we as teachers talk with our students about beginning a book and then deciding not to finish it?

Who Reads Ahead?

As readers, we differed with regard to reading ahead in a book. We got onto this topic when Marybeth Harris, a third-grade teacher, told us about reading *A Map of the World* (Hamilton, 1994). She said, "It's really good. This woman's life is just a mess. It is so chaotic, and she's so disorganized. She can't relate to her children. She wants to be a good mother, but she loses things, her house is dirty, and her kids are screaming." The way she described this story led us once again to laughter.

It was in telling us about the title of the book that Marybeth got to the issue of reading ahead. Alice, the woman whose life is a mess, trades baby-sitting duty with her best friend. The book begins with the friend dropping off her two children. Alice goes upstairs to look for a bathing suit because she and the children are going swimming in the nearby pond. In a dresser drawer, she comes across a map of the world she drew when she was a child, and her mind drifts while looking at the map. She comes out of her daydreaming and rushes downstairs only to find that the 2-year-old child is missing. She looks all over the house. Marybeth said, "My heart was pounding as I was reading. I had this sense of disaster from the beginning just from the way she was so disorganized. You just know something is going to happen. So she goes to the pond and finds the 2-year-old floating facedown. She can't remember how to do CPR, and she's a nurse. But she tries anyhow, and then she gets a doctor and they take the child to the hospital. It goes on page after page, and you don't know what is going to happen to the child. I had to look ahead; I just could not stand the suspense. I had to know."

As we discussed reading ahead, Vicki Hanson, an early intervention program teacher, was reminded of her experience reading *Where the Heart Is* (Letts, 1995) because it was for her one of those books that you can only enjoy if you read the ending and know that everything is going to end up all right. Like Vicki, Marybeth said she often reads ahead because that makes it possible for her to go back and enjoy the story more. Vicki also skipped ahead in *The Red Tent* (Diamant, 1998) but for a different reason. She chose to read it because she has read several books by another author, Francine Rivers, who is a Christian fiction writer. Rivers writes about people in the Bible that Vicki likes very much, and Vicki thought *The Red Tent* would be along the same lines. "It's very different," said Vicki with a laugh. She did not want to stop reading it, but she had been skipping ahead because she found the middle of the book "a little slow." She commented that this skipping ahead was evidence that she was interested even though the book was not at all what she had expected or wanted.

The discussion led Jill to say that she would feel guilty reading ahead, which led me to wonder aloud if we are taught implicitly in school that the right way to read fiction is to begin at the beginning and read word by word and sentence by sentence to the end—to read in a linear fashion. Betty B. brought forth another perspective when she said there are good reasons to read a book all the way through and not skip ahead. For her, "it's a hopefulness, a reverence for the process." She remarked, "I would not cheat myself of what the writer has built up for me."

Yet there are authors who encourage us to read differently. Annette Santana, teacher educator at the University of Georgia, told us about reading David Egger's *A Heartbreaking Work of Staggering Genius* (2000), a story about a 24-year-old guy who becomes the parent to his younger brother. The author tells the reader that he or she can skip around from chapter 1 to chapter 4 to chapter 3. Annette found that "he keeps it light," even though he's telling about awful experiences, such as his mother dying of stomach cancer. Some writers apparently write in a way that keeps in mind that not everyone reads linearly.

In sharing our own experiences with reading ahead and not reading ahead, we were led to acknowledge different reading realities. When do we want to read ahead? When do we skip around in the text as readers? When do we read with reverence the order of words the author has crafted for us? How often do we as teachers talk about this with students?

Got a Reading Friend?

After our first session as teachers who read, Tricia Bridges, a third-grade teacher, visited a teacher friend of hers who has a whole room full of books. Her friend helped her select several books to borrow—ones that she had enjoyed and thought Tricia would enjoy, too. She began with a mystery story, *The Guardian* by Dee Henderson (2001). For her it was "one of those you just do not want to have to close, but you have to go to bed because you have to go to work the next day."

Hearing about Tricia and her friend with a room like a bookstore, Betty Hubbard (Betty H.), instructor at the University of Georgia, was reminded that "there's something really special about a friend of yours giving you a book and telling you they can't wait for you to read it so you can talk about it."

In the previous session when Margret told us that reading *When Bad Things Happen to Good People* was challenging her beliefs, Betty B. had commented on the importance of having someone you can talk to when you read

> "[T]here's something really special about a friend of yours giving you a book and telling you they can't wait for you to read it so you can talk about it."

and find yourself in one of those troubling reading situations. Betty B. talked appreciatively of having a special friend or group of friends with whom it feels safe to admit that something you are reading is disturbing.

As teachers, do we know which of our students have special reading friends? Do we know if our students go to reading friends to talk about what they read that challenges or troubles them? Do we know if they have someone to whom they can recommend a good read? Do we invite conversation about having a special reading friend or friends as part of teaching reading? How does one find a special reading friend? Should relationships and reading be part of current national and state standards for reading language arts?

Who Is Reading What?

As a group, we were becoming reading friends. Our process of coming to know one another as readers and teachers was helped along by our practice of writing on the whiteboards around the room titles and quotations from the books, newspapers, and magazines we were reading. As we sat in a huge semicircle of desks looking at red, green, blue, and black colored writing on the whiteboards, perhaps others were like me in feeling pleasure when a title seemed to step out from the crowd saying, "Remember me?" It was like one of those happenstance meetings with someone you are really fond of but have not seen in a long time. I just had to tell Vicki and the others that I had read *The Red Tent* and just that day I had carefully wrapped it for a long journey to Botswana. I was sending it to be shared among three women who I was quite sure would find the author's feminist tale of Leah, daughter of Jacob, an interesting story.

For Marybeth, recognizing a title was somewhat different. She was "curious to know who is reading *Ellen Foster*" (Gibbons, 1987) because she had the book at home and had never read it. Several of us said, "That's a good story," but it was Margret who had put the title there for us. She told us that it was

> amazing all the references that are made to Ellen Foster's reading life. She talks about reading all the time. Ellen reads

all the time so her mind won't ramble—so she can make her brain shut off because her life is hard.

We all seemed to know about reading as a way to leave our present reality to enter into someone else's reality or to go somewhere beyond our present concerns. We would return to reading as escape, or solace, three weeks later when we met a week after September 11. We shared what we were reading to learn about the world each session until our seminar ended on December 4, 2001. We continued to take pleasure in seeing that someone had read something we had read, and we continued to be curious about what one another were reading. It was pleasurable, it was interesting, and it was educational.

Are our students given time and opportunity to be curious about what their classmates are reading? How much do our students know about the personal reading lives of their classmates? What connections exist among our students when it comes to their reading lives? Is knowing about other people's reading, particularly the reading done by family and friends, important enough to be a standard for reading and language arts? Can it be a standard if we cannot test it?

Did You Cry?

As noted before, at the beginning of each seminar session we wrote quotations from our week's reading on the whiteboard at the front of the room. We also wrote the titles and authors of what we had read or were reading. The whiteboard was full most weeks. It gave us a point of departure to talk about our reading lives.

One week, Sarah Bridges, a fifth-grade teacher, offered us the quote, "She had no more water for tears." During Drop Everything And Read (DEAR) in her fifth-grade classroom, she had read that sentence in *Cane River* by Lalita Tademy (2001, p. 166). She shared with her students how sad she felt when she was reading. On that school day, Sarah had invited them all to complete the statement "When I read this morning, I felt...."

Sharon chimed in: "I cried. Tears were rolling down my face." Sharon had stayed up all of a Friday night reading *Before Women*

Had Wings by Connie May Fowler (1996). She was entranced by the story, as told by a little girl, about a very special family with lots of problems. Sharon was going to tell her students about her all-nighter with a book because she wanted them to know how caught up with a book she could get.

I wondered aloud if our students would be surprised to know that their teachers sometimes read and weep. I could not recall for sure the first time I was moved to tears by a story. I do remember fighting back tears almost three decades ago when strict Mrs. Estes read us E.B. White's (1952) *Charlotte's Web* in third grade.

Sarah said that just that morning during DEAR time, her students were watching her read and asked, "What happened in your book?" They had noticed her facial expressions as she read and were curious. Sarah was not even aware that she was being expressive or being watched. It was as if they were watching signs of comprehension that led them to want to know what her book was about.

Barbara thought it was good for her students to see her cry. Sympathy for characters is why reading matters to us. There are a couple books she reads each year that she has to call on another teacher to finish because they are so sad for her that she cannot manage reading aloud. She explained, "I don't think they perceive me as being foolish. They just learn that I am softhearted about some things."

Once, Marybeth had told her students about something sad in her book. She was astonished when a girl said, "Listen to this." The third grader read aloud from a book about Johnny Appleseed. Johnny's father goes off to war, and Johnny's mother and baby sister die. Marybeth said her students were very quiet as they listened. The girl then flipped to the end of the book and read about how Johnny gets sick and dies after never being sick a day in his life. The third grader looked up from her reading at everyone in the class. Marybeth said this was a departure from the students' usual focus on plot and events. She commented, "I think it's happening because I'm starting to share my reading more with them."

What Is Reading for Pleasure?

I observed that the phrase *reading for pleasure* was often used during the seminar. I wondered about that because my reading is often nonfiction, and mostly when I heard the other teachers talking about reading for pleasure, they meant fiction, that is, novels. I let everyone know some of the questions I was wondering about, and asked, "Does reading for pleasure mean it is joyful?" When Sharon read all night and wept at the end of *Before Women Had Wings*, was that pleasure?

Betty B. said, "I think if we have an intention about a book—if we are true to a book—then we are reading for interest."

That reminded me of a preservice student of mine who told our class that she had decided to read a book she had tried earlier in life because now she thought herself more mature and ready to read it. She was reading C.S. Lewis's *The Screwtape Letters* (1982), and it was difficult, but it was good. She was determined to finish it, even though it was not a total pleasure for her. As her teacher, I was pleased to hear about her commitment to reading Lewis.

Marybeth had her own Lewis reading experience. She recalled reading *Mere Christianity* (1958), and it was also difficult, but it was "so interesting the way he explained things that you just got into it." She felt that if something was interesting, then it could be called reading for pleasure.

Jennifer Olson, graduate student and instructor at the University of Georgia, was also rereading. For the third time, she was reading Joseph Heller's *Catch-22* (1961). She told us,

> For some strange reason, I picked it for my book club. I didn't want to read it anymore, but I had chosen it. I felt a commitment to read it to the end. And in the end, it was worthwhile because I saw the different views that people brought. It didn't speak to me the way it spoke to other people. If I hadn't finished the book, I wouldn't have seen what they saw. But it was not a pleasure to reread that book. I don't know if it was ever a pleasure even the first time.

After listening to the students' thoughts on reading for pleasure, I wondered aloud, Do our students realize that sometimes we—their teachers—read things that are hard for us? Do they know that sometimes we persevere and why we persevere? And sometimes we don't persevere. It might be important for us to tell our students about reading we do that is hard but worthwhile. It might be interesting to them to learn that our rereadings can span 10 years. I'm excited thinking about these things that we can talk about with students because they come directly from being more in tune with ourselves as readers.

> *It might be important for us to tell our students about reading we do that is hard but worthwhile.*

Should I Read a Really Big Book?

At the beginning of the seminar, Barbara told us that she really wanted to read the new biography of John Adams by David McCullough (2001). She had been carrying it around with her but was undecided about whether to read something that would take months. "What will your students think when they see you lugging that big book back and forth to school?" I asked. Barbara replied, "They'll think, 'She's a really slow reader'!"

Barbara's dilemma seemed related to something I'd been pondering for awhile. I told the students,

> I'm concerned that the consumer- and productivity-oriented society we live in is leading us to have a consumer orientation toward reading. What I mean is that we think reading more and reading faster is better. But reading to get through a book so as to get on to the next book does not encourage savoring.

Betty B. asked, "And how is that played out in schools with Accelerated Reader?" Accelerated Reader is a commercial reading management program in which students read only those books that have an accompanying computer-based comprehension test. Sarah thought her students had learned that the length of their list of books they had read was most important. This issue also comes up in writing workshop, where children are very concerned with how many pages they have written. Lori said that the time it takes to read a long book was influencing her planning. When she went to the library to check out books for her third graders, she found herself skipping over chapter books because it would take three months for her students to read them. Jill remembered teaching third graders who thought "the kids who had the biggest books were the coolest in the class."

I let Barbara know that I was excited that she wanted to read the John Adams biography because then she could tell us about it. She started reading it during the seminar and sent us all an e-mail message when she completed the book after the seminar had ended.

Are You a Born-Again Reader?

Debbie Barrett, a middle school language arts teacher, told us about reading an essay from *On Lies, Secrets, and Silence* by Adrienne Rich because her daughter was reading it for a freshman English course in college. Also, Debbie was attracted to the essay's title "What Does a Woman Need to Know?" (1979). She thought it was going to be juicy, but it wasn't. It was an address Rich gave to a women's college about education. Debbie said it was a tough read and not a pleasurable read.

Debbie's reading of what her daughter was reading got Vicki wondering how it would be for parents of younger children to read what their children were reading. She saw potential for both child and parent in sharing and talking about the same literature, not reading the selection together, but individually, and then talking about it. Vicki thought it might get parents to read more often and give children a new perspective on their parents as readers and thinkers. Vicki's musings led Debbie to tell us,

> I'm a born-again reader. There was a long spell when I did not read at all except for magazines and newspapers. I didn't read books. I thought fiction was useless. I read nonfiction for information—self-help books. But when my daughter was in middle school, my mother-in-law got her hooked on Mary Higgins Clark books. They are suspenseful. She was reading them like crazy. I kept thinking it odd that she was so turned on to books, and here I was not reading at all and I'm a teacher. My daughter kept encouraging me to read her books, so she was the one that got me back to reading fiction five or

six years ago. And I did enjoy having that communication with my daughter. We could always have an all-night book talk.

> "Books can become common zones that get parents and children into meaningful conversations."

"That's a great story," I said. "Have you ever told it to your seventh-grade students?"

"No," Debbie said with a laugh.

"Books can become common zones that get parents and children into meaningful conversations. Think about telling your students about this," I encouraged.

Debbie did, and what happened is the focus of her essay in this book (see page 142).

Are You a Newspaper Reader?

Lori told us about a three-part article she found in the *Augusta Chronicle* about the Tubmans (Wynn, 2001). The article told the story of how a group of slaves freed by Richard Tubman in 1836 traveled to Africa with the help of his widow, Emily, where they settled in a colony that eventually became Liberia.

I asked, "Are you a newspaper reader?"

"Always have been," Lori replied. "That's one thing I remember about my dad. He was not that educated of a person. He barely graduated from high school, and he did not like school, but he loved to read the newspaper. He didn't read books. He would read magazines, and he would read the newspaper."

"Was your mother a newspaper reader?" I asked.

"She does look at the newspaper, but my dad reads everything in the paper," Lori explained.

Vicki said, "At my house, it's the opposite. My mom reads the paper every day."

Renèe added, "My dad reads the paper constantly. I love to read the paper, too. So it's kind of interesting that it's fathers and daughters."

"It seems that the habit of newspaper reading is something picked up at home, not at school," I suggested.

Tricia said, "I don't read the paper at home, but when I visit my mom, we'll sit down and read the paper. I do it there, but I don't do it at home."

Renèe explained, "My dad and I talk about a lot of things if we've both read the paper, especially editorials. We get a conversation going, and it's fun."

In our discussing who was a regular newspaper reader and how that came to be, we found another way in which reading creates conversation among family members. Jennifer wondered about what was happening with the programs in which newspapers are donated to schools. It seems that making the most of those donated newspapers depends on whether the teacher is an avid reader of newspapers. How could we re-create in classrooms the newspaper readings that Lori and her dad shared, that Renèe and her dad shared, that Tricia and her mom shared? What if students read newspaper articles at school and then went home to find that their fathers or mothers had also read those articles? One could imagine the conversations that would happen as child or parent asked, Did you read the article about such and such today?

How Did September 11 Affect Our Reading?

We met one week following the terrorist-led plane crashes in New York, Washington, D.C., and Pennsylvania. We agreed to write about how reading made a difference for us since September 11 and then talk about what we had written.

Betty H. wrote the following:

Since September 11, I have become increasingly cognizant of the centrality of reading to my life. Reading is both the essence of who I am and what I can become.... In a sense, I become what I read by trying on the premise of various authors as though their thoughts, words, and values were garments.... I searched online for news and discussed events with relatives in other countries. I am eager to know how the Afghans live—the plight of women and children. There has been no escape. My thoughts have turned toward the mindset of others—those I know well and those who are unfamiliar. I wonder what they believe.... Reading is how I make sense of the world.

Margret told us,

> "Reading is how I make sense of the world."

Because of last Tuesday, I picked up a book that I had put down. Not long ago, I was having trouble reading *When Bad Things Happen to Good People*. I had started reading it originally because my little girl was asking all kinds of questions after the death of my aunt. A rabbi wrote it, and I just felt like he was trying to change my faith in God. But I went back and read some of the things I had underlined.

Margret had put a quote from the book on our whiteboard: "Only human beings can find meaning in their pain" (p. 86). She told us, "I wonder how I let myself be so illiterate and ignorant about world issues. It brings to mind that ignorance is bliss."

Debbie relayed to us that she had been reading the Bible. The verse "Be still and know that I am God" kept resounding for her all week. "I feel like in the midst of all the confusion, I have just needed to be still. But I also felt really guilty reading anything except information [about the attacks]."

With everyone sharing how their reading lives were affected by the events of September 11, it was apparent that in some ways, we used reading similarly to get information—to learn more about the world. There was also significant variety in what we chose to read. It was interesting to talk about the role of reading in our lives during that historic moment. It makes me wonder about times past. What role did reading play in my fifth-grade life when John F. Kennedy was assassinated? What role did reading play in my ninth-grade life when Dr. Martin Luther King, Jr. was assassinated? I do not recall being encouraged in school to read my way through those times of confusion and despair. I do not think my teachers told us about the role reading played for them during those times of national disasters. In retrospect, I think it would have interested me. It would have encouraged me to know that reading was one way of making sense, of finding solace, of knowing how to go on.

We have written our stories as readers who teach and teachers who read. We have read our stories to one another. In thinking across these stories of what we had learned by spending just 15 weeks being a community of readers and teachers, we were inspired to introduce the idea of stances to accompany the standards for teaching reading. This you will find as the conclusion of our book.

REFERENCES

International Reading Association. (2000). *Excellent reading teachers.* A position statement of the International Reading Association. Newark, DE: Author.

Wynn, M. (2001, September 2). Untold stories. *Augusta Chronicle*, p. 8A.

LITERATURE CITED

Childress, M. (1993). *Crazy in Alabama.* New York: Putnam.

Diamant, A. (1998). *The red tent.* New York: Picador.

Eggers, D. (2000). *A heartbreaking work of staggering genius.* New York: Vintage Books.

Esquivel, L. (1994). *Like water for chocolate.* Englewood Cliffs, NJ: Prentice Hall.

Fowler, C.M. (1996). *Before women had wings.* New York: Putnam.

Frank, K. (1986). *A voyager out: The life of Mary Kingsley.* Boston: Houghton Mifflin.

Gibbons, K. (1987). *Ellen Foster.* Chapel Hill, NC: Algonquin Books.

Hamilton, J. (1994). *A map of the world.* New York: Doubleday.

Heller, J. (1961). *Catch-22.* New York: Simon & Schuster.

Henderson, D. (2001). *The guardian.* Sisters, OR: Multnomah.

Karon, J., & Nelson, D.K. (1999). *The Mitford years: At home in Mitford/A light in the window/These high, green hills/Out to Canaan (Vols. 1–4).* New York: Penguin.

Kushner, H. (1981). *When bad things happen to good people.* New York: Schocken.

Letts, B. (1995). *Where the heart is.* New York: Warner Books.

Lewis, C.S. (1958). *Mere Christianity.* New York: Macmillan.

Lewis, C.S. (1982). *The screwtape letters.* New York: Bantam.

Lowry, L. (1993). *The giver.* Boston: Houghton Mifflin.

MacMillan, T. (2001). *A day late and a dollar short.* New York: Viking.

McCullough, D. (2001). *John Adams.* New York: Simon & Schuster.

Rich, A. (1979). *On lies, secrets, and silence.* New York: W.W. Norton.

White, E.B. (1952). *Charlotte's web.* New York: HarperCollins.

—Betty Shockley Bisplinghoff—
TEACHER EDUCATOR

Betty is an assistant professor in the Department of Elementary Education at the University of Georgia. Her path to this position has been full of memorable teaching in primarily urban public school settings. For the past 17 years, she has had the honor of teaching and learning as a teacher of kindergarten (1983–1988), first grade (1988–1993), third grade (1996–1998), and sixth grade (1998–2000), and as director of the School Research Consortium at the University of Georgia (1993–1996). She earned her undergraduate degree from the University of North Carolina at Chapel Hill and her Master of Education and Doctor of Philosophy degrees from the Department of Language Education at the University of Georgia. When Michelle Commeyras told Betty about her plans to create a graduate seminar class for teachers that would be codesigned by participants and focused on reading choices and discussion, Betty became a member of the class, even though her schedule was packed with the demands of being a new professor. Michelle asked her to cofacilitate the class, and Betty could not have been more pleased to begin her tenure track with such an exceptional experience.

When reconsidering the reading she did during the semester of the Readers as Teachers and Teachers as Readers seminar, rather than highlighting a favorite text, she remembered an insight she gained about herself as a reader. Her reflections from Monday, September 3, 2001, include the following:

> I'm laboring through the book BEE SEASON (Goldberg, 2001). Jill loved it and read it quickly. I, on the other hand, am losing interest. I think it's because of the tedious victim mentality of the family members. They are so unable to find productive ways to improve their day-to-day life experiences. This is very contrary to my way of looking at the world. Does this mean that when I read something that demonstrates little or no agency on the part of the primary characters, that I reject the text? An interesting exploration might be to list the books I've loved alongside those I've cast off. I wonder what more I would discover about myself as a reader, thinker, and doer.

CHAPTER 2

The Reading Life: It Follows You Around

Betty Shockley Bisplinghoff

Recently, I had the pleasure of observing one of my student teachers performing a dramatic reading of *Caps for Sale: A Tale of a Peddler, Some Monkeys & Their Monkey Business* (Esphyr, 1947) with her pre-K–K class. As I watched the unfolding of this experience, my mind wandered and wondered about the relationship between being a book lover and the peddling attitude I have for supporting teaching from a more authentic stance. I hope I can explain how this attitude enlivens how we live, how we read, and how we teach.

Beginning with the events of the pre-K–K classroom I was visiting, I celebrated the value of time devoted to playing with text. I watched the students become physically and emotionally engaged by this classic tale about a peddler walking from site to site, day after day, with a varied load of caps to sell, all of which are balanced precariously, yet colorfully, on top of his head. As the story unfolds, one afternoon, weary from his wanderings, the poor peddler stops to rest in the shade of a single tree and is soon asleep. He awakens sometime later only to discover that he is capless. As folk tale luck would have it, the tree that offers him respite from his daily task also happens to be the favored gathering spot for a group of mischievous monkeys. The monkeys are presented in the illustrations quite humorously because each is wearing a new cap plucked from the peddler's stack. As each page is read aloud to the students by the intern, the adventures of the peddler and the monkeys are given life by these pre-K–K actors. The preferred scene of the young students listening to the tale was obvious as they anticipated the confused awakening of their classmate who was playing the peddler character, the opening of his eyes to see them all wearing the caps that once had been atop his head. More fun ensued as the illustrations of the monkeys mimicking the peddler's appeals for the return of his goods are presented and the students interpret the process by stomping their feet like the peddler does and eventually throwing the caps supplied as props by their teacher on the ground just like the peddler in the picture does in his final act of frustration. This desperate action miraculously generates the response that nets both the storybook peddler and the student peddler the return of their wares. The children were joyous and seemed satisfied that all is once again well and good as the peddler is able to continue on his way and carry out his life's work. I, however, was left with an altogether new spin on the situation. I reconsidered the part where the peddler throws his hat on the ground and receives the benefits of an unexpected response from the monkeys. Could it be that as soon as the teacher throws his or her cap into the ring as a real reader, so to speak, the students will do likewise? Is there something here to inform my wonderings about the value of students and teachers being actively involved with texts, making connections back and forth between text and life's work?

It is a stretch, I understand, to consider the plight of the peddler in such direct association with teaching and learning, but I would like to engage this image as a point for attending to what I perceive as a sad situation in schools today, a situation in which teachers are peddling the current culture of schooling without realizing that students are watching us and mimicking our behaviors, perhaps seeing things we don't mean for them to see. When students mimic our actions, what will that look like? What view of reading, for instance, are we modeling? If we take risks, will they? This concern became more and more of an issue for me as I participated in our Readers as Teachers and Teachers as Readers seminar and heard my teacher friends proclaim that once students got past the pre-K–K stage, there was little time in the curriculum to learn through story; there were standards, pacing guides, and schedules to keep.

> Could it be that as soon as the teacher throws his or her cap into the ring as a real reader, so to speak, the students will do likewise?

I worry that in my zeal to promote more authentic practices in schools—to think of myself as a learner, to design more meaningful learning opportunities for me and for my students, to develop memorable literate relationships with my students, to take professional risks—I step on other people's feelings. For instance, the first time I tried on the new professional cap of researcher, I wanted it. JoBeth Allen, professor in the Department of Language Education at the University of Georgia, pointed this role out to me. She wore her cap, figuratively, when she came to observe students with me in my classroom, and I wanted one, too. For me, researcher was the piece that had been missing in my professional wardrobe. I've come to realize, however, that this is not the case for all teachers. Some see this new cap and think they can't afford to add one more thing to their already overwhelming workload. Others have the desire but don't want to pay the price of questioning and the awareness this may bring. Of course, there are also those who just never liked the idea of wearing hats at all and seem content with business as usual—capless and exposed to gusting winds of change.

To extend my worries about becoming an insensitive zealot and selling my ideas without thoughtful consideration of other viewpoints, I try to keep in mind how each of us is shaped by the current cultural expectations in the places we work and that we also act as shapers of that culture. To continue shaping my tale of concerned confusion, I bring into view the peddler as myself and wonder about how I look to others. I begin exploring this case by referencing the influence of yet another storied example, *Walking Across Egypt* (Edgerton, 1987), also one of my favorite books.

Edgerton's main character, 78-year-old Mattie Rigsbee, worries over things like I do. She is a hard worker, even though, because of her age, she is necessarily slowing down. Mattie actually is beginning to take a few liberties regarding local expectations:

> She had gotten into the habit of not washing her dishes right
> away after lunch. She waited until..."All My Children" was
> over at two. Nobody knew. If anybody ever found out that she
> both watched that program and didn't clean up right after she
> ate, she didn't know what she would do. But after all, things
> did happen in the real world just like they happened on that

program. It was all fiction, but anybody who read the paper nowadays knew things like that were happening all the time. (p. 8)

All was fine with Mattie's clandestine routine until one fateful afternoon when she decides to remove the bottoms of her chairs for reupholstering and forgets about this detail when she moves to sit, relax, and watch her show:

> She had started sitting down when a mental picture flashed into her head: *the chair without a bottom.* But her leg muscles had already gone lax. She was on the way down. Gravity was doing its job. She continued on past the customary stopping place, her eyes fastened to the New Blue Cheer box on the TV screen, her mind screaming no, wondering what bones she might break, wondering how long she was going to keep on going down, down, down. (p. 10)

Once she finds herself safe yet totally stuck within the confines of the remaining chair frame, she panics:

> Lord have mercy—what if Alora [her best friend] comes in the back door and sees me watching this program? What in the world will I say? Well, I'll just say I was sitting down to watch the news when I fell through, and so of course I couldn't get up to turn off that silly soap opera. That's what I'll tell her.
>   Then she will see my dishes stacked over there.... (p. 11)

As time ticks by, the ultimate worry presents itself to Mattie, "What if she *died* one day during the hour her dishes were dirty? She would have to change her routine" (p. 12).

When I was growing up, I knew many women like Mattie. They held themselves to locally contrived standards, questioning only how well others were living up to the given codes of conduct but rarely challenging the sources or broader worth of such long-held habits. I distinctly remember my aunt talking about how her new neighbors were suspect because they did their laundry on Sunday and even hung the clothes out to dry so everyone could see they were not very Christian folk. The "real" Christian folks responsible for supporting my informed passage into their community—my family—hired a series of wonderful black women to care for me on a daily basis while they went to jobs outside our home. Through the years, I observed these "other mothers" (Collins, 1991) of mine singing their Christian hymns as they matter-of-factly completed household tasks and watched over me. I rode to town sitting snugly at the back of the city bus beside them.

Linking a scene from literature and the scenario from my own living, I entered the world of teaching with a wondering attitude and found potential to use this attribute to my advantage and for my students' benefit as I routinely questioned my practices, especially in terms of what was merely habit or tradition versus what was a possibility. The years of combining teacher research with teaching kept me also enrolled in graduate classes until finally, one amazing day, I graduated with the culminating degree, a Doctor of Philosophy degree. Just recently, I was hired as an assistant professor at the same university and as fantasy-job luck would have it, discovered that my friend, Michelle Commeyras, was initiating a new graduate seminar focused on the possibilities of being a teacher who reads. My dissertation addressed this issue, and I was eager to participate. Michelle welcomed me and suggested we could cofacilitate the class meetings.

Here's where that peddler tendency sneaks back into my illustrations of pivotal experience: During the first few meetings of our seminar, it was all I could do to be a listener and not interject my opinions. I actually wanted to fall through my chair—not to be stuck like Mattie, but to escape the tensions I was feeling. Here we were all well-meaning people, just as my parents and extended family had been. I could tell that everyone cared deeply for her work and deeply for her students. It just disturbed me that so many seemed so sure, reminding me of the acceptance of custom (when to do dishes or laundry) and even law (certain people must ride at the back of the bus) that allowed members of my family to reject people and ideas that were different from the way their world was ordered and to support separate status for the women with whom they entrusted the care of their child. I'll try to explain more by using a

> *I entered the world of teaching with a wondering attitude and found potential to use this attribute to my advantage and for my students' benefit.*

few segments from transcripts of our class meetings as well as excerpts from my after-class written reflections.

During one of our early September class discussions, a class member burst forth with the comment that she'd never shared her reading with her students and had "never even considered it!" I was momentarily dazed by this unexpected revelation that such an essential aspect of my classroom practice in support of engaging students as readers could be so previously unthinkable to another classroom teacher and graduate student in the reading department. Soon, I heard other teachers begin to consider possibilities for their reading to matter for their students:

Teacher A: There were some things I could have shared from *Ellen Foster* [Gibbons, 1987], which I just finished. She was a child, and I think they would have enjoyed hearing some of the things I read. But I kept forgetting to take it out there [to school]. But anyway, I just shared with them today or it may have been last week. I told them that I read every night—that was my homework, except that I didn't have a certain book to read. I got to pick what I wanted to read. And they thought that was really neat. Then I told them, I was talking to them about reading out loud because with remedial reading when you go through a guided reading lesson, you do a lot of reading out loud, and I got to thinking when I was reading my book, I thought they probably get so sick of it because you have to listen to the ones that are really struggling. They all have to sit through that. And you can tell the ones that get aggravated while they're trying to listen to this other child just plod through. So I said to them, "I thought that I would hate everything I had to read if I had to read it out loud, so today you're just going to get to read your book by yourself." I felt kind of funny about doing that because they're probably not going to read if you're not standing over them making sure they're reading everything, but they just looked up to me with relief in their eyes. They were so glad they didn't have to read out loud. They were so excited. So they got to just read, and I was walking around and said, "Now you are going to have to read some to me just so I can see how you are doing." This one child who really has been having so much trouble reading out loud, I thought, he can't be in the third grade having this much trouble with reading. He couldn't have gotten this far with that much trouble. But he did so much better today, and I guess it was the reading in front of the other children [that was] worrying him. He did so much better, and I felt so much better. But they were just so excited. And they said, "We really enjoyed doing that, can we do that again?" I said, "We can't do it every day, but I promise you'll get to read some things silently." They stayed on task. I could tell they were reading. And so I was just very pleased with that because I expected them to just flip pages and say, "I'm through," in about two minutes. And they didn't. They really stuck with it. So I feel by sharing with them kind of how I feel as a reader about things, I think they would really appreciate that.

Michelle: That's a wonderful example of how just thinking more about yourself as a reader gave you a new idea and a new sensitivity for their situation as readers.

Teacher B: I did that also. I work with the same kinds of kids at my school. And, I decided to let them have some silent reading time. I would read and [I told them] at the end of this if you want to talk and share your book please feel free.... They all wanted to share, and then they wanted to go get another book and do it again. I told them we

would try and do that. We can't do it everyday
but...we could work it into our schedule.

Once again, I actually thought I would fall through my chair
on hearing teachers talk so casually and unquestioningly about
how their current classroom practices must take precedence over
their students' desire to "really" read. I could see them worrying
like Mattie that they would be caught with their dirty dishes in the
sink if they did read silently every day or allowed students to
choose their own books to read. This could be like watching a soap
opera instead of a more acceptable news program. I ached over
how their adult reading had the potential to make such a lasting
difference for their students in terms of seeing these significant
adult models really using reading as a source of pleasure and
information rather than as monitors of a particular reading
program—something that changes with each textbook adoption
cycle. I tried to temper my peddling reaction with the following
approach:

Betty B.:   Can I ask a weird question?

Michelle: I don't see why not.

Betty B.:   Why can't you do that every day?

Teacher C: We have certain things—a format we have to use—
and EIP [the early intervention program] kind of
sets this: It's the guided reading part, and then the
making words part. And each day...a little journal
time, so you'd have to cut out that.

Michelle: How often could you do it?

Teacher C: Probably twice a week. Sometimes, they take
books home and read them and bring [them] back
and share a little bit each day. And we write down
how they did readingwise. Sometimes, I'll cut out
that part and let them read silently.

Betty B.:   So you found the part that you cut out because
you didn't think it was as valuable as the reading
silently part?

Teacher B: Right. Right.

Betty B.: So it's a feeling of if you don't do what's set out there, you get behind?

Teacher C: With us, we use one Big Book for the whole week. And we do different things with the book. And so each day has something to do with the day before. So if you get off track, by the end of the week, you might not have done all that you can do.

Teacher A: I have three third-grade groups, and one of them is not as far along as the others. So you know with one group, I'm really having to do more guided reading because they're so far behind. But I have two other groups; they're fairly much on grade level, so with them I'll be able to do more. But I have to do grades, and I'm responsible for their assessment and things. With that one group, I've really got to try [to] boost them a little bit more, so I won't be able to do it as much.

At this point in the discussion, I just wanted to fall asleep like the peddler and wake up to a different reality. I worried about those children's faces that looked up at the teacher with such relief at having the opportunity, finally, to read books they wanted to read and not to have to read out loud. I feel sad that this teacher has gone through all her schooling, all the way to graduate school, before she has been offered the chance to read from sources she chooses. Tempering my strong reaction to the seminar discussion, I wrote my reflections:

> Funny—when I got home, the kitchen table was laden with catalogs from the day's mail. My only reading that night was these catalogs and my *Southern Living* magazine, which also just arrived. A wonderful smile came to my face as I turned a page, however, and saw in the book review section *Ava's Man* (2001), the new Rick Bragg book we discussed in class. Ahh—the reading life—it follows you around!

"Ahh—the reading life—it follows you around!"

I started thinking again about my dissertation study. I spent two years studying my thinking and decision making as a language arts teacher in a middle school. One of the key understandings gleaned from this effort was the importance of reading as a way to see beyond the requirements of my local setting. I read to find out about the history of curriculum development in the United States. I read to find a community of authors with whom I could mentally interact and create basically a virtual professional community. Ultimately, I came to see reading for information and for pleasure as a profound way to strengthen one's sense of professional character, a way to develop an informed professional voice. Without choosing to be a reader who teaches, I would have been hard-pressed to find the support I needed to become my own kind of teacher. I was thinking about how easy it was to decide there's not enough time to read. If I didn't have a high degree of confidence, based on my self-study, that the decision to make time for reading would benefit me (both emotionally and professionally), it would be harder to make the effort. We all just always seem to be so busy.

Piling all these experiences and ideas *in* my head rather than on top, like so many peddler's caps, does not make as obvious a statement about the balancing act that we all participate in as we try to make sense of our professional situations and our personal lives. I am reminded that we are each negotiating our own autobiographies as we participate in what D. Britzman calls the "institutional biography" (as cited in Florio-Ruane, 2001, p. 26) of our school sites. In addition, Britzman contends, "whereas role can be assigned, the taking up of an identity is a constant social negotiation" (p. 26). As participants in the Readers as Teachers and Teachers as Readers seminar, some of us were placing ourselves in very new territories and renegotiating roles as teachers.

Then came the session in which Michelle chose to read out loud to us from the book she had been reading during the previous week. Her reading took me to more new territories. The power of commonly accepted culture hit me again. I was reminded that sometimes it takes something out of the ordinary to interrupt the balance of caps (understandings) we have worked so hard to achieve. Michelle chose to read from Paul Theroux's travel writings, *Fresh Air Fiend: Travel Writings, 1985–2000* (2000):

The Mouse Missions of the Pashwits

Among the Pashwits, a pastoral people in central Asian Turkestan, the ability to carry a live mouse in one's mouth for a great distance without harming the creature is regarded as an essential skill, acquired in the passage from boy to man.

A Pashwit boy becomes a warrior by feeding flesh from his own body to the mouse, and once the mouse is fattened in a way that impresses the commander of the Pashwit army, it is eaten.

The male organ in Pashwit is also known as a mouse. Pashwit women are forbidden to look at a mouse or even to utter the word. (p. 444)

The Cat Totems of Moto Tiri

At one time, all over Oceania, dogs were raised to be eaten, and still are in many places. Dogs are also found in the meat markets of Southeast Asia and throughout China. Instances of cat-eating are rarer, chiefly occurring in Alotau, in Milne Bay in New Guinea, and in some outlying islands in the Philippines.

But in Moto Tiri cats are universally eaten, and every part of the cat is used—its meat forming a significant source of the islanders' protein, its fur used as decoration, its bones fashioned into needles and hair fasteners, its teeth into jewelry. The cats are wild. They feed on the island's dwindling bird population.

Butchered cats are displayed in Moto Tiri markets—the legs, the haunches, the back meat; some are sold dressed or stuffed. They are coated with sauce, they are smoked, and some are salted. Cats are the essential ingredient in stews; they are fried, poached, and baked; they are served *en croute* with taro crust.

I mentioned to a man in Moto Tiri that cats are house pets in much of the world. He laughed at such a novel concept, and in the course of our conversation I learned that pigs are the house pets of Moto Tiri. They always have names, and are petted and made a fuss of. They are never eaten. On chilly nights, pigs are often taken to bed by the natives and embraced for warmth, a practice that has given rise to the affectionate name for a pig on the island, being called "a Moto Tiri wife." (p. 446)

Of course, we listened intently to these "odd" behaviors and practices, finding it difficult to imagine that others could live so differently from us. There was the tendency to think that these were descriptions of long-ago habits. We were even more shocked to learn that these observations occurred between 1985 and 2000. At the conclusion of her sharing, Michelle did not address the issue of culture. The intent of her introduction of this material into our discussion was to highlight the variety of genres from which we could choose. My mind was, nonetheless, whirring with connections to things we do in our schools every day that others might find odd. How long did it take us to question how we presented information to our students about Christopher Columbus, for example? So many things we take for granted as givens. What other things are we doing that could benefit from more questioning? Who made the decision that it is better for struggling readers to spend one whole week with one big book that children may not find interesting, instead of facilitating the development of perhaps the most essential reading skill of all—learning to choose good books for yourself? How important is it for students to learn to spend a different kind of extended time with text? How do we show the value of learning how to be alone with a book and letting your mind experience the work and pleasure of making sense of reading? I remember the night that Sharon shared with us how she read all night. She said, "I cried. Tears were just rolling down my face. [I read until] about six o'clock in the morning. I read all night long. I didn't put it down. I thought, 'Oh, this is so delightful. I feel I'm doing something bad 'cause I stayed up all night to read.'" How did we grow to think reading all night, something so delightful, could be bad? What is the origin of the underlying guilt we seem to feel when we choose to read for pleasure in school and at home? All this makes me think of the character Mattie again. I bet she only puts certain kinds of books and periodicals out for the anticipated neighborly review, too. Do we teachers prepare for principal visits in a similar way?

We are all caught in "webs of significance" (p. 3) that Clifford Geertz (1973) defines as culture. Elizabeth Chiseri-Strater and Bonnie Sunstein (1997) explain that "culture is a slippery term.... Every group has a culture.... We define culture as an invisible web of behaviors, patterns, rules, and rituals of a group of people who have contact with one another and share common languages" (p. 3). Our schools operate as special cultural settings. As participants in that culture, we are the ones who give shape to the behaviors, patterns, rules, and rituals that exist there. Just as practices have been instituted, so can they be deconstructed and reconsidered by us. Like the peddler who offers his caps for sale, I'm beating a path toward a more authentic view of reading and teaching in schools. I'm hoping to sell more people on the idea that aspects of reading that adults hold dear may likely be the very same things that will help students become attracted to reading and make them want to spend their time in pursuit of the written word. I'm throwing my cap in the ring and hoping like heck that many others will, too.

> *I'm beating a path toward a more authentic view of reading and teaching in schools.*

REFERENCES

Chiseri-Strater, E., & Sunstein, B. (1997). *Fieldworking: Reading and writing research.* Upper Saddle River, NJ: Blair Press.

Collins, P.H. (1991). *Black feminist thought.* New York: Routledge.

Florio-Ruane, S. (2001). *Teacher education and the cultural imagination.* Mahwah, NJ: Erlbaum.

Geertz, C. (1973). *The interpretation of cultures.* New York: Basic Books.

LITERATURE CITED

Bragg, R. (1998). *All over but the shoutin'.* New York: Vintage Books.

Bragg, R. (2001). *Ava's man.* New York: Knopf.

Edgerton, C. (1987). *Walking across Egypt.* Chapel Hill, NC: Algonquin Books.

Esphyr, S. (1947). *Caps for sale: A tale of a peddler, some monkeys & their monkey business.* New York: W.R. Scott.

Gibbons, K. (1987). *Ellen Foster.* Chapel Hill, NC: Algonquin Books.

Goldberg, M. (2001). *Bee season: A novel.* New York: Knopf.

Lamb, W. (1996). *She's come undone.* New York: Simon & Schuster.

Theroux, P. (2000). *Fresh air fiend: Travel writings, 1985–2000.* Boston: Houghton Mifflin.

—Sarah Bridges—
FIFTH-GRADE TEACHER

Sarah was a first-year teacher during the course of the seminar Readers as Teachers and Teachers as Readers. She taught fifth grade. She took on a graduate course while beginning a new career and appreciated the learning she experienced from her own reading as well as from discussions with other teachers. She felt that it is important to convince teachers to try to share their reading lives with students.

Sarah's favorite reading during the seminar was THE POISONWOOD BIBLE: A NOVEL by Barbara Kingsolver (1999) because when she read it for the first time, she began to get excited about words and writing in general. While reading, Sarah would write down all the words she thought were fun to say and use, like "hootenanny," and then she would share them with her students. That reading experience was fun and new, and Sarah became amazed with Kingsolver's writing abilities. Since then, she has read three of Kingsolver's other books. This was the first time Sarah began to like an author on the whole and not just a single book by an author.

CHAPTER 3

Mexican Hair: Was the Answer Right in Front of My Face?

Sarah Bridges

"All right readers, on the count of three, I want you to call out the title of the book you are reading. Don't be shy. Use those powerful voices, like Martin Luther King, Jr.'s voice when he said 'I have a dream.' One-Two-Three: *The Poisonwood Bible*!" I roared into the tumult as I shared the title of the book by Barbara Kingsolver (1999) that I'd been reading. "Now, after the third count this time, scream the name of your favorite character in that book. Use one of those screams of excitement, you know, like the kids use when they find out they all passed their standardized tests and their school wouldn't shut down in Dr. Seuss's [1998] *Hooray for Diffendoofer Day*. One-Two-Three: Leah!" My shout blended with the blast of voices of the enthusiastic young readers. I continued by saying,

> Your favorite character is in mind. Now prepare for a
> visualization experience. Take your right hand and cover your
> eyes completely. Think. Your character is trapped inside your
> head and can't come out because your eyes are closed. So
> concentrate.... Are you caught in a swarm of feeling,
> appearances, and amazement about the complexity of your
> character?

Hoping that at least one person pretended he or she saw her character in his or her mind, I waited. There they sat, 10 students in an oval on the floor, eyes closed, mouths open, waiting for a chance to speak. Each student knew he or she must wait until he or she heard no other sound before delving into a description of the chosen character's wily ways of thinking, outrageous outfits, or enviable intelligence. The art of turn taking that we'd been practicing was a skill not yet perfected. Still bodies waited, rather impatiently, while a few fingers were called away from their duties as blindfolds. Sneaky eyes demanded a peep.

Someone broke the silence. "I see him now. He has Mexican-style hair, and he likes to comb it a lot." Immediately, my ears caught the sound of muffled giggles emerging from the mouths of a few children near me. Amazingly, all eyes remained closed with the exception of mine and those of two Mexican American students, one whose hair was short with a blond highlight accenting his brown fluff, and the other whose hair became progressively longer as it reached his forehead. "What is Mexican hair?" the three of us with our eyes open seemed to wonder in silence. We, and now everyone else, looked around at the other Mexican American students in our class and, I assumed, all recognized that not one even had a similar style of hair to another. All eyes but mine snapped shut as I squeezed my brow, as a reminder to return to looking into our minds, not out to one another. Another student continued with his interpretation of his author's description of his favorite character. I, now only partially listening, contemplated how I could quickly contrive a question that would, I hoped, initiate conversation about this Mexican hair thing. I knew I would *have* to inquire.

A few minutes later, after the excitement of sitting in an oval with our eyes closed and only speaking when someone else was not, the room turned silent and we opened our eyes. Our debriefing of this new process began with my attempt to respond to the happenings so far, "You know, sometimes when I am reading a book, I really want to ask the author what she meant by something she wrote. Well, that is how I feel right now. I really want to know, what in the heck is Mexican-style hair?" Those whose eyes had been slow to open were now sitting up straight and looking as if they might never blink again. My nudge had been successful.

A few students seconded my question. "Yeah, what is that anyway?" The reader of *The Watson's Go to Birmingham—1963: A Novel* by Christopher Paul Curtis (1997) tried to

"[S]ometimes when I am reading a book, I really want to ask the author what she meant by something she wrote."

explain that Curtis meant that Mexican hair was slicked back. She knew that because the author wrote that in the very next sentence. Almost simultaneously, the student gathered data with her eyes about the hair of her Mexican American classmates and mumbled, "But I wonder *why* he called it Mexican-style?" The conversation grew into a confusing and insightful dialogue about Mexican hair, white hair, black hair, and all hair. It ended with an agreement that it was inaccurate to say that all people who share a culture have the exact same appearances, preferences, and feelings. Of course, in the terms and expressions of 10-year-olds, our conversation's culmination sounded more like, "Yeah, it just isn't right"; "That's just bootleg"; "It'd be like someone sayin' that we all *love* Elephant Gerald [sic] just because that is what Ms. Bridges loves and we're all in her class." "Yeah," the 10 heads nodded in agreement, reinforcing the fact that they all, in fact, did not love the music of Ella Fitzgerald as I did. It also heightened our awareness of hair, and we spent the morning exploring different authors' descriptions of characters' hair, including Sandra Cisneros's description in *The House on Mango Street* (1994), a book I had read a few weeks earlier—a huge discussion for an event that wasn't even planned.

The morning of the Mexican hair incident, I certainly did not write in my plan book, "Today we want to understand what a Mexican's hair looks like according to Christopher Paul Curtis's book *The Watson's Go to Birmingham—1963: A Novel.* I will tell them about my experiences with Mexican's hair, and then we'll talk about what an Asian's hair looks like and so on. We might even compare [others' hair to] our own hair." In my planning book for this day, I actually wrote the following:

> If we begin to discuss the characteristics of our characters, we will not only be learning about how authors write with detail but also how we feel about the way authors write to let us in on the thoughts of their characters. Do we necessarily have to agree with the way an author describes a character? Shouldn't we practice the skill of questioning what's around us? Isn't reading a way to question our beliefs? Get them to think!

"Do we necessarily have to agree with the way an author describes a character?"

Granted, I *had* purposely preplanned to guide this group, who usually read about immature characters like Junie B. Jones and Hank the cowdog and their inane conflicts that were almost always completely resolved by page 100, toward reading *The Watson's Go to Birmingham—1963: A Novel* because I hoped it would make them want to talk or write about their feelings provoked by a more serious text. They would not be able to quietly accept how characters that may be similar to them are described or the extreme hatred occurring in days when Jim Crow stereotypes were overtly present.

But still, I hadn't planned for a student to bring out racial and ethnic stereotypes in the middle of reader's workshop, or had I? I knew someone was bound to feel uncomfortable once this text was discussed, but how much influence did my familiarity with book discussions influence the thoughts and responses of the students in my classroom? Was I more willing to encourage students to talk, write, think, and question authors because that is what I was experiencing in my own reading life?

As a first-year teacher, I decided to overwhelm myself even more by starting graduate school. My first course focused on how reading related to teaching and vice versa. So as part of my coursework and in an effort to build a reading and writing community with my students, I began doing the same homework as my fifth-grade readers each night. I read for 30 minutes, then wrote about it. I turned in my homework to my students, and they had the opportunity to respond and ask me questions. I remember that at the beginning of the year, this whole experience was rocky, but I suspected that sharing this reading was somehow important. I decided to review the data to better link my teaching work with my learning work as a student. I started at the rockiest part—the beginning of the year.

I collected data from various sources. Two sections on my self-designed planning template required me to state the reasoning behind my intended goals and actions and reflect about the outcome of my lessons. In addition, anecdotes on sticky notes and scraps of paper, transcripts from taped discussions on teaching and reading, conference records from reading and writing workshops, checklists on reading behavior, and student-designed rubrics littered my desktop at home. Quickly, I became a teacher desperate to understand herself and her students. And just as quickly, I ran smack into a new wall in my thoughts: My reading life was undercover.

I had started the year expecting that the plans I'd anguished over as my first ever in my teaching career would be so powerful that after the first few days, my reflections would contain phrases like, "Wow, we all love to read in here," and "Boy, it sure is great to be with a group of thinking readers." But I didn't find that. My planning template looked more like the following:

> **Goal (Before Teaching):** It's the third day of school. Ask students to tell about themselves as readers. I want them to realize that they are readers and that they have something to tell. I also want them to start thinking of themselves as readers who think.

> **Reflection (After Teaching):** Students write about selves as readers for approximately three seconds. Their responses more or less say, "I do not like to read. Reading is boring, and it takes too long. I am not even good at it." My response is one of frustration and confusion, "We aren't excited! How can we become more excited? Perhaps we will be when we get books we love. Or maybe it's that I am not reading aloud everyday. I'm sure that is it."

The next day, my template showed the following:

> **Goal:** How can we start to enjoy reading and writing? We must find personal space while we listen to books we love or might love. I will read *A Bad Case of the Stripes* by David Shannon (1998) because students might relate to a character who has a lot of feelings. I want them to know that there is nothing wrong with feeling when you read.

"We must find personal space while we listen to books we love or might love."

> **Reflection:** Did they listen? The students' responses largely resembled the following: "My tummy hurts." People are

talking. Burp. Squeak. Ruffle, ruffle through pens and pencils. Smack, smack, smack of gum. Feet rustling, constant tapping, book bags unzipping. Perhaps it was not the book to get kids excited. We will find our own books tomorrow.

My mind was filling with frustration, but everything seemed like it should've been so smooth. I was doing the right things according to what I'd remembered from my reading classes in college. I met all the criteria of the checklist in my mind about the things a good reading teacher does. I chose to read aloud a book that one of my professors had read to my undergraduate class. I was planning and thinking about what readers might like. I was looking at the students' responses and asking myself, What were you thinking? I was asking and expecting students to become readers. I was requesting that students learn with me—oh wait, maybe this is it. I was not involving myself as a reader in our learning process. My reading life was certainly buried under a pile of confused thoughts advocating one right way to teach reading. I had to do something to provide space for my reading, too; however, I didn't know where to start, so I continued as planned.

> **Goal:** Introduce reading baskets as personal space for our own books. Perhaps owning the tools for reading will help us own our reading.
>
> **Reflection:** Students watched as I read *Cane River* by Lalita Tademy (2001) during Drop Everything and Read (DEAR) time. They didn't move a muscle except those in their eyes as they watched my eyes tear. I was reading about a character's grief over her dead children and lost husband. I mentally threw my lesson plan out the window, and a new plan emerged as students questioned, "Ms. Bridges, are you OK? What happened? Why did that book make you cry?" Times like this, I want to kick myself in the foot for not listening to every person who has told me that if I want students to read and love it, it would help to see someone else reading and loving it. How can I expect them to think and feel about characters and ideas when possibly no one around them, or at least at school, openly reads for many purposes? Maybe I should come out as a reader.

After this breakthrough day in which my students saw their teacher as a reader and not just a person who talks about reading but not about her reading life, my goals as a teacher-learner-reader came out for us all to see. My central literacy planning questions evolved into (1) How can the students and I understand the effects we allow books to have on us? and (2) How can we change the environment to support a love of evaluating literature and investigating the feelings we have when we read?

Until then, I had not revealed myself to be a reader, but on this day my response to literature emerged as a physical manifestation. I reached a point in my book where I just *had* to get in touch with feelings and thoughts, and it seemed to start a trend. I had chosen to read, respond, and let it be known to the students that I was not the least bit ashamed of finding out more about myself as a reader. Now I had to try my hardest to give my students the same opportunities to unearth their knowledge about reading. They needed the same comfort I felt. They needed experience thinking and talking about books so they could evaluate their reading and develop the skills and confidence to respond authentically. But how could students jump from thinking, "Huh, why would we want to read a book and respond to it when we can easily bypass the thinking and just take a recall test on details?" to "Are you kidding? You mean you only read so that you can take a test? What a waste of time!"

When did I start thinking this way? Why? How? Would understanding these things about myself help me make better decisions in support of my students? Was the answer right in front of my face? Had I found it? I had started looking at myself as a reader in order to support my students as readers. After all, the whole confusing incident about reading and responding seemed to emerge from my surge of emotion-filled reading. Let's just say, however, this was not exactly something I was jumping to do. I was a nonfiction teacher-reader. I read for information. I wanted to know how other people did things. Could I really convince a group of children that reading is the "coolest" by plopping down with a pile of books with titles like Lucy Calkins's *The Art of Teaching Reading* (2000) or Robert Reys and colleagues' *Helping Children Learn Mathematics* (2002)? Not only was my genre list quite unimpressive but also the only books the kids had seen me touch so far were those professional books that I had on my classroom shelf. I'd pick them up occasionally and flip to a page or two, but I never sat down to read them. Did my students think that my fumbling and stumbling through books was the only kind of reading adults did? Did my moment of tears with the character in *Cane River* really shock my students that much?

I started to get nervous. I began to question my capabilities and myself as a teacher of reading. Don't children need a consistent model reader? Wouldn't it be better to leave my crazy reading life out of the picture and find a guest teacher-reader, a person who would be the perfect model reader and who wouldn't mind hanging around the classroom until May? Could I really just explore with my students the reader I am, as well as the reader I want to be? I *had* experimented with reading in the presence of my students. I *had* released my insecurities about the questions my reading led me to ask of myself. And in revising my approach to teaching reading by including my learning within the framework, I *had* watched my connections to literacy and my students grow. Did I need to be so concerned?

Within a week, I disclosed a new goal to read more in various genres, and I began to turn in my reading-response journal to my class with hopes of eliciting more response. As I grew as a reader, I shared my stories and strategies. As I opened up, I became more confident with the strategies that I already had as a reader of mostly nonfiction. The more confident I became, the more I shared. The more I shared, the more the students shared.

> Could I really just explore with my students the reader I am, as well as the reader I want to be?

I told of how sometimes when I read, I would breeze through a page of a book and have no clue of what had just happened in the story. Many students revealed that they often had the same trouble. As a class, we developed a question to ask ourselves in case we felt our concentration slipping, "Huh, what was I reading?" Pretty soon, I could hear the question around the room as students checked their comprehension and others' by asking the new question, "Hey, what are you reading?"

As I brought more of my books to school, students started questioning my technique of marking the pages with sticky notes. Sure enough, sticky notes were soon missing from the writing workshop supply station in astonishing numbers. These sticky notes seemed to aid our discussions when questions of understanding arose. So naturally, I began to change some of my planning so having time to think independently and with others about reading and what readers do and recognizing the importance of doing so became necessities every day.

Quickly, our reading and writing journals began to transform from "My book is about blah blah blah" to "I can't believe that character did that! I would never do that!" Our discussions became more alive as we even devoted entire days to reading and talking about books. As our new thinking and reading lives grew more complex, so did the ideas and issues that we discussed in our reading community. More and more, I read and recommended books on complex issues and ideas and added my comments to book talks, such as the following:

> You know, when I read this part in Lois Lowry's *Number the Stars* [1998] last night where an older female character told her brother that she didn't know how he could stay alive without a woman to cook and clean for him, I got really mad. I sat right down and wrote about it. I wanted to know how a few sentences got me so mad. I wrote about how I didn't think it was fair for the woman to act like only women can cook and clean, like that is the woman's job or something and the men shouldn't have to do it themselves. Anyway, it's in my homework notebook if you want to read about it.

Another day, I commented,

> I just read a book about Rosa Parks and what she did. The author, Herbert Kohl [1995], found that she had planned the whole sit-in on the bus ahead of time. And she had refused to move on many other buses before and been arrested many times. She wasn't the tired little lady who just happened to find enough strength to decide not to lose her seat on one single day, even though that is how she is presented in some biographies.

More and more, the students began to read more complex books and their comments also grew in complexity:

> I was reading *The Rainbow Hand: Poems About Mothers and Daughters* by Janet S. Wong [1999] last night, and I was pretty sad by what I was reading. It reminded me of something sad that happened in my life. I had to sit down and write about it, too.

> Did you ever wonder why when Mildred Taylor [in *The Gold Cadillac*, 1987] writes about white characters she usually says things like, "the white man," but when she writes about the black characters she doesn't often say they are black?

> Why didn't that white family take help from the black family in *Bud, Not Buddy* [Curtis, 1999]? They were all starving.

> I read in the newspaper last night that Osama Bin Ladin [*sic*] is Muslim. Kara in Mr. Smith's class is Muslim. Does that mean she wanted all those people to die in the plane crashes?

> I feel tricked by what Jean Fritz [in *Shhh! We're Writing the Constitution*, 1987] says sometimes. I don't want to be tricked anymore.

Slowly but steadily, sitting comfortably on the floor in an oval, the responses we had to our authors' choices and how all the stories related to our own lives became second nature. These discussions began to drive our actions in class. For instance, in response to a student not wanting to be tricked by authors, we generated a list of things some readers think about when they read so they won't be tricked. At the top of the list was the simple question, "Why should I believe the author?" This led to a list of "tight topics for book talks"—topics such as connections we felt with the characters and taking time to question whether we agreed with something a character did or said—which we used in discussions. Thinking and questioning even made it to our list of qualities of good writing. And after listening to tapes of a few of our own book talks, we even decided that we did not need to use the traditional roles of literature circles, such as discussion director, who asks the questions, because we seemed to do those things naturally without the specific jobs.

Slowly, my students and I became readers who shared, responded, questioned, and read in various genres. By investigating and trying to understand where our reading community began and where we are today, I have come up with even more questions. I cannot stop thinking about how far we should or should not go. Is it enough to think and question what we read, or should we also evaluate what we believe through our reading?

In the seminar, Michelle asked one day, "How did [your students] respond to the shattering of the romanticism of the children's biographies of Rosa Parks?" I brushed over the issue at the time. I said they were excited to think more about reading and not be tricked by authors any more. Now I think, How did they really respond on the inside? How uncomfortable they must have felt, knowing that something so many people had told them in the past was not necessarily the true story. I felt pretty uncomfortable reading one of Herbert Kohl's essays in *Should We Burn Babar? Essays on Children's Literature and the Power of Stories* (1995). Is feeling uncomfortable the only way to become thinkers and readers?

> Slowly, my students and I became readers who shared, responded, questioned, and read in various genres.

What I believe about education and learning is that learners do need to experience a level of discomfort when presented with new information. They feel uncomfortable because the new knowledge goes against what they currently understand and know. For instance, mathematically, if a student knows only to use her fingers to add numbers, when she is asked to add seven plus five, she will have to adapt her current understanding of numbers and fingers to find a place for the extra two. In reading, it is not as clear-cut. The end results of reading a book are not as definitive as mathematical concepts. One can easily read the words on a page and not create an ounce of meaning from what is read. As I described earlier, I've been preoccupied as a reader at times and needed to go back and reread a page or two because I never truly processed the words. Still, it is even easier to read the sentence "He loved his Mexican-style hair" without thinking twice about my current thoughts on Mexican-style hair and how all people from Mexico do not have the same hair.

When we meet in the oval, talk and write about books openly, and question others, aren't the students and I scaffolding one another's learning? Aren't we questioning the very concepts and ideas that might have remained covered without such sincere communication? Hasn't understanding been my planning goal all along?

If I had not planned to have a discussion after the students' and my experiences with Mexican hair, perhaps the idea that the description felt uncomfortable to some of us would have only remained in the open for a second. If we had not planned time to talk about our responses to our characters' descriptions, if I had not recommended *The Watson's Go to Birmingham—1963: A Novel* to a group of students, if I had not ditched my original plans on the day that the students first noticed my response to some literature, if I had not responded openly to *Cane River*, if I had not read *Cane River*, or if I had not read at all, would the students and I be as thoughtful about our reading as we are today?

REFERENCES

Calkins, L.M. (2000). *The art of teaching reading*. New York: Longman.

Kohl, H. (1995). *Should we burn Babar? Essays on children's literature and the power of stories*. New York: New Press.

Reys, R.E , Lindquist, M.M., Lambdin, D.V., Smith, N.L., & Suydam, M.N. (2002). *Helping children learn mathematics*. New York: Wiley.

LITERATURE CITED

Cisneros, S. (1994). *The house on Mango Street*. New York: Knopf.

Curtis, C.P. (1997). *The Watsons go to Birmingham—1963: A Novel*. New York: Bantam.

Curtis, C.P. (1999). *Bud, not Buddy*. New York: Delacorte Press.

Fritz, J. (1987). *Shhh! We're writing the Constitution*. New York: Scholastic.

Kingsolver, B. (1999). *The poisonwood bible: A novel*. New York: HarperCollins.

Lowry, L. (1998). *Number the stars*. New York: Dell.

Seuss, Dr. (with Prelutsky, J., & Smith, L.). (1998). *Hooray for Diffendoofer day*. New York: Knopf.

Shannon, D. (1998). *A bad case of stripes*. New York: Blue Sky Press.

Tademy, L. (2001). *Cane river*. New York: Warner Books.

Taylor, M. (1987). *The gold Cadillac*. New York: Dial Books for Young Readers.

Wong, J.S. (1999). *The rainbow hand: Poems about mothers and daughters*. New York: Margaret K. McElderry.

—Lori Whatley—
EARLY INTERVENTION PROGRAM TEACHER

Lori has been teaching elementary school for eight years. She began teaching as a Title I teacher for first-grade reading and math. Since then, she has been a reading specialist for kindergarten and first, third, and fourth grades, working with students in small groups.

Her favorite reading from the Readers as Teachers and Teachers as Readers seminar was SLEEPING AT THE STARLITE MOTEL: AND OTHER ADVENTURES ON THE WAY BACK HOME by Bailey White (1995). She enjoyed this book because it showed the importance of story in our lives and allowed Lori to tell her stories in her own voice.

CHAPTER 4

That's How My Students Feel!
Lori Whatley

I't's one of our family get-togethers. The kind where all the female adults try to visit and have a civilized conversation while the children are running wild and the male adults are mad because they are trying to watch some type of ballgame and they can't hear the television. Between fussing at children, complimenting the cook, and cleaning up dishes, the question is eventually asked, "Have you read...?" It's as inevitable as Uncle David's stories and Aunt Rannie's picture taking. I sit and listen, a wave of jealous heat washing over me, wishing I had more time to read. The lively discussion continues, and I make mental notes about which book I would like to read next if I could find the time. As a teacher, mother, wife, daughter, and graduate student, reading for pleasure is usually one of those activities saved for *the* week at the beach.

Every year, I search for the perfect book, one about which I can say, "Oh, it's to die for" and join in the conversation of "Have you read...?" I usually find what I am looking for before we leave for vacation. I make the annual trip to the local Borders, waltz in like I am someone with a frequent-reader card, hang around the various specialty tables, read the backs of books, and sip espresso to give the illusion that I am a regular. I buy the book and then leave it lying on my bedside table to gather dust. When *the* week arrives, I place the book in my beach bag very carefully as if it were a recently discovered buried treasure.

Flash forward—it is *the* week at the beach with the same family, all 21 of us. Needless to say, I am unprepared. No preemptive trip to the bookstore has taken place—no time. How disappointed I am as I stand in front of the measly bookrack at the Jekyll Island Pharmacy. Where are the Oprah Book Club selections or some of the novels I read reviews of in the newspaper? I want something deep and profound, full of meaning that will leave words like stamps imprinted in my brain. Not that I don't enjoy a fast read every now and then, but I want to read a book where I know the characters and understand their situation, where I see myself reflected in the author's words and images. I don't usually choose books about unfamiliar things because I know there will be no connection there, no way to apply meaning to my life. As I reflect on how I choose books, I think of my students and how they feel as they look for books to read. In the media center or the classroom library, are they standing there thinking, "Is this all there is? Is this what I have to choose from?" Do they walk away as disappointed as I do?

Before the Readers as Teachers and Teachers as Readers seminar, I never gave much thought to my reading behaviors—how or why I chose a certain book to read, or why I simply quit reading a book after a few chapters. After being given the choice to read whatever I wanted (because that was the assignment for the seminar), I began to think more deeply about who I was as a reader and as a teacher of reading. I have decided that these two lives are not separate; one greatly enhances the other. The teacher of reading's life will suffer if the personal reading life is ignored. I have experienced this in my own teaching and now feel so guilty for the injustices I have served on my past students. I am ashamed to say that I did not allow my students to see that I took part in reading or let them know that it was something that meant the very world to me. I did not share my experiences as a reader. I did not share the joy I felt when completing a long book, the satisfaction as I turned the last page and absorbed the last paragraph, not wanting to finish but not being able to wait. I never shared the frustration of picking out a book that I thought would be so wonderful, only to be disappointed enough to shut the cover, never to return again. I never told them that I, too, had to read certain passages more than one time to understand what was happening and that I had to look words up in the dictionary to see what they meant. I did not even ask them to tell me about a book they were reading. There had been no dialogue about why we chose certain books or about behaviors that readers have. In general, teachers (myself included) seem too busy to teach the fundamental reading behaviors that good readers possess. We assume that students already have these concepts, when in reality they truly don't. The concepts are not part of our quality core curriculum (QCC) objectives, so I never thought to take time to teach them to students.

The teacher of reading's life will suffer if the personal reading life is ignored.

Why am I realizing only now that students need to know that teachers of reading actually have a reading life outside of teaching? I have been teaching for seven years, so surely I learned this in some staff development! No! For the past six years, I taught first grade and felt very confident that I was meeting the needs of all the students in my classroom. I was proud to watch my students grow into fluent readers when only months before they couldn't remember sight words, to note their names disappearing from the at-risk report, and to see their reading scores continue to climb toward the 1.5 benchmark required for promotion in our county. Even Elvis would have been proud; I was T.C.B.—taking care of business!

Now I am teaching third grade. Eight-year-olds are so different from 6-year-olds. What had always worked in first grade might not in third, so I felt a little lost as I planned what was best for my students. As many teachers do, I had tried to follow in the footsteps of the teacher before me. She used books of high-interest stories with controlled vocabulary. She taught guided reading lessons using these books and seemed to have great success with this method. What's good for the goose is good for the gander, so I decided to give it a try. I was prepared at the beginning of the year to teach my heart out—the kind of teaching you read about in Vivian Paley's books, in which everything is just so darn perfect, teachable moments are abundant, and teaching hypnotizes students so they don't even realize they are learning. So imagine my dismay when I pulled out the little bag of books and the students said, "Oh no, not those again!" "We did those last year." "We did those with our tutor." "Those are baby books." "When are we going to read something hard?" I tried to remain enthusiastic throughout the day as I taught my third-grade groups, but each time, the reactions were the same. I could not keep going. There was no motivation and certainly no engagement in their reading. I had students falling asleep, playing with their pencils, flipping pages, and reading ahead of other group members. "I am in teacher hell," I thought. I was desperate, so I started giving the students daily participation grades, and each time they were not looking at the book, staying on the correct page, or paying attention, their grade was lowered 10 points. The participation grades worked for about a week. After all, who cares about a good grade as long as you can do something entertaining and not pay attention to something you were not interested in?

Thankfully, relief was in sight! I had to test students using the computer, one student at a time. While I worked at the computer with one student, I allowed my other students to color a book about the United States. It was shortly after September 11, 2001. I couldn't believe how busy they became, making their books, writing, and worrying about how to spell words and if what they were doing "looked good." As I talked with a colleague and shared my experience, she suggested the students write their own stories and then swap with other students to read them. We both agreed this would be more motivating than reading the simple little books over and over.

A plan began to form, but I did not really have a starting place. As students began to write their own stories, I realized they could not write even a simple paragraph. I wanted to find some way to teach them the basics of paragraph writing, but I wanted to do something fun, some "way cool" activity that would just throw them for a loop and make them say, "I can't wait to go to Mrs. Whatley's class today!" Any reaction is better than eye rolling and heavy sighing. I tried to borrow other teachers' ideas about teaching paragraph writing, but their ideas did not quite meet my expectations of the three-ring circus I wanted to use to entertain and educate my students. As any technologically talented teacher adhering to House Bill 1187 (Georgia Governor Roy Barnes' A-Plus Education Reform Act, which brought sweeping changes in funding, class size, teacher qualification requirements, student achievement, and accountability to public schools) would do, I searched the Georgia Department of Education Learning Connections website. I found an idea for teaching students to write paragraphs, all hands-on activities, and nothing *boring*! The students' reactions were astounding. One student asked, "Are we going to read those little books again?" I told her that I didn't think so and that I thought they were tired of them; a whole room full of eyes shined up at me and almost simultaneously, a resounding "Yes!" echoed across the room complete with the cha-ching arm motion. Several girls ran up, hugged me, and said, "Thank you, thank you, thank you! We love you Mrs. Whatley!" I asked the students if they liked the writing and if they would like to continue doing writing activities. The students actually seemed amazed that I cared to ask their opinion about what they wanted to learn. I doubt I would have asked the students their opinion in the teacher-who-never-read-days, but after reading a quote in *Ellen Foster* by Kaye Gibbons (1987), I could no longer pretend I was the teacher who knew best. Ellen says,

> I can hardly tolerate the stories we read for school. Cindy or Lou with the dog and cat. Always setting out on some adventure. They might meet a bandit or hop a freight but the policeman or engineer always brings them home and they are still good children. (p. 9)

These words leapt off the page and slapped me in the face! "Why, that's how my third graders feel," I thought. How many of my third graders were like Ellen and can "hardly tolerate" what they were reading? Then I remembered how I felt in third grade, reading round robin in my group. I was in the top reading group and grew up in a home where reading was a priority. I never struggled with reading. It was something I just did naturally. I remember feeling like the reading we did out of those basals wasn't real. Real reading was what I did with the books that my mom ordered for me off the book order or when I read the newspaper with my daddy. Did my students see the reading at school as not being real? Ellen did see it that way, and even though she had no literacy support at home, she continued to seek solace in books. Perhaps that was her motivation and salvation. She said herself, "I

The students actually seemed amazed that I cared to ask their opinion about what they wanted to learn.

am not able to fall asleep without reading. You have that time when your brain has nothing constructive to do so it rambles. I fool my brain out of that by making it read until it shuts off" (p. 10).

Books about taking a pet to the veterinarian don't mean much in my students' daily lives, I'm sure. Just as Ellen's choice of reading at home was much different from the choices dictated at school, it is no different with my students. They told me so. How many times do teachers encourage students to talk about their reading material at home, and how many times are these choices validated? I bet I can count them on one hand. I deal with the issue that my students may be escaping their world through reading. It is real, and my reality and the reality of the school is not their reality at all.

While I was reading *Ellen Foster*, I wondered how Ellen overcomes the obstacles of her home life and learns to read so well that she could read an encyclopedia. Where does she find the motivation to go to the library and check out books, use the services of the bookmobile, and discuss great works of literature with the librarian? Many of my students come from families where school is not a priority or where one or more family members are not literate. So many of them live in situations like Ellen's—a sick mother who eventually dies and an alcoholic father who isn't around much, the child thrown from family member to family member, not knowing where she will sleep that night or the next. In these situations it is no wonder students aren't interested in the texts they read at school. They have so much else on their minds that as they try to read words unconnected to them, they simply get lost. As a teacher, I had always thought they were not listening, but now I realize this is the exception, not the rule. I myself don't choose to read books about subjects I don't like or understand, so how can I blame these students? I no longer feel I have to be the one doing all the teaching and imparting my wisdom as if it were the only kind of wisdom there is to have. I am involving the students more and making my reading classroom more child-centered.

In trying to grow and change as a reading teacher, I asked my students what else they wanted to do in reading. Each group wanted to read the stories that the other students in their classrooms were reading out of the literature-based reading series. They wanted to read what they were missing while working with me. The week we began working on two stories about spiders, students were so interested and engaged you could have heard a feather fall on the floor. They almost fell out of their desks trying to answer questions and share all they knew about spiders.

Another book, *Evensong* by Gail Godwin (1999), also affected my life as a teacher who reads. One character, Dr. Sandlin, is headmaster at a boarding school for troubled adolescents. When discussing his thoughts on education he says,

> Young people aren't being given the necessary minimum of intangibles to grow on. They suffer from psychic undernourishment. Wisdom is developed in young human brains by the curriculum of conversation, thought, imagination, empathy, and reflection. Young people need to generate language and ideas, not just listen and watch as passive consumers.

These words of wisdom aren't from a reading research guru but a fictional character. How true they are! When I read this quote, all my concerns about how at-risk readers are taught came flooding into my brain. Politicians, administrators, and even teachers feel that at-risk readers must be taught using a heavy skills-based curriculum in order to drive test scores to all-time highs, which is simply not true. At-risk readers need authentic opportunities to use language, both oral and written, to make improvements. Just as Dr. Sandlin says, students need many opportunities to participate in conversation, to engage in reflection, and to use their imaginations. What better way to accomplish this than by reading and talking about books?

Other teachers, administrators, and even parents may view this as wasting time, but I can think of no better way to build a love of reading and tap the reservoir of motivation just waiting to overflow from all students. I know standardized test scores are important in my job as a Georgia educator. The age of accountability

At-risk readers need authentic opportunities to use language, both oral and written, to make improvements.

is here to stay until the pendulum swings again, but I know I can't
begin to address objectives and be successful until I have first
developed a relationship with each student. If I don't, I have no
credibility as an adult eager to make a difference in their lives, and
I will only seem like another grown-up trying to impose my middle-
to upper-class standards on them. I am so grateful for the
opportunity to build successful relationships with my students.
Stephen Covey, author of *The Seven Habits of Highly Effective
People: Restoring the Character Ethic* (1990), says a successful
relationship occurs when emotional deposits are made to the
student, emotional withdrawals from the students are avoided, and
respect is given to students. He also notes that the primary
motivation for students' success will be in their relationships. High
test scores are secondary, but they will improve as a direct result of
teachers bonding with children. Knowing that I am building strong
relationships with my students makes me feel confident that I can
help to bridge any reading gap they possess.

As I continued my personal reading journey, I again asked
students for their input on what they wanted to learn. My only
criterion was that it had to help them progress as readers. Together we
had a discussion about how students viewed themselves as readers.

I allowed each student to discuss his or her strengths and
weaknesses and how he or she defined reading. I was amazed at
students' mature, thoughtful responses. One student said, "I have
trouble figuring out hard words, and I don't understand what I read."
Several others nodded their heads in agreement. No one laughed or
teased; all were sensitive to their classmate's dilemma. I shared with
them the objectives that I was required to teach and my high hopes
for them as readers. The discussion served as the turning point in
our student-teacher relationship. I noticed the difference it made
when I shared what I was reading or writing or if I told them of an
assignment I had to turn in. They couldn't believe that I had to take
a "big test" (a comprehensive exit exam) to graduate.

The camaraderie the students and I now share after
discovering one another through our discussions is priceless. It can
bridge any gap they possess in the area of reading. Now they are
more respectful of me and put forth the extra effort to complete

work and participate in class. I am more understanding of their needs as readers and as people, not just some warm bodies taking up space in my classroom. I no longer view them as fill-in-the-bubble machines but as human beings in search of meaning and how they fit into our school culture. I appreciate their differences and how their individual personalities contribute to our learning community. It took a few months, but I feel as if I am right on track to help these third graders acquire a lifelong love of reading. I can honestly say these changes wouldn't have occurred without my reading books for pleasure and thinking about the ideas I read in relation to my classroom and my life (which are many times one in the same). I also look forward to the next family get-together because this time I will be the one asking "Have you read...?" and I'll betcha 10 bucks they haven't!

REFERENCES
Covey, S.R. (1990). *The seven habits of highly effective people: Restoring the character ethic.* New York: Simon & Schuster.
Georgia Department of Education. (1999). *Georgia learning connection's teacher resource center.* Retrieved from http://www.glc.k12.ga.us/trc

LITERATURE CITED
Gibbons, K. (1987). *Ellen Foster.* Chapel Hill, NC: Algonquin Books.
Godwin, G. (1999). *Evensong.* New York: Ballantine.
White, B. (1995). *Sleeping at the Starlite Motel: And other adventures on the way back home.* Cambridge, MA: Perseus.

—Marybeth Harris—
THIRD-GRADE TEACHER

Marybeth has taught for 20 years. She began teaching first and second grades and then took time off to raise four children. Since returning to teaching, she has taught first, second, fourth, fifth, and seventh grades. She is currently teaching third grade.

Her favorite reading from the Readers as Teachers and Teachers as Readers seminar was I KNOW THIS MUCH IS TRUE by Wally Lamb (1998) because it tells an incredible story of twins, one of whom is schizophrenic.

CHAPTER 5

"They're All Reading in There"

Marybeth Harris

I sometimes think it has always been this way. It fits so naturally into the daily flow of my classroom. I look forward to it, but then I remember this is an exploration, not an experiment. To call it an experiment sounds so cold and analytical, and it is neither. It is warm and comfortable—Read-Share-Read!

My third graders bounded into the classroom predictably at 11:45 a.m. daily, full of lunch and limitless energy. The schedule, written by me, read "SSR (sustained silent reading): 15 minutes." Nothing new here; it's done every year. But this year, this time, I was going to attempt to curl up in my comfy chair with my own good book for the entire 15 minutes. I was going to forget that I was their teacher for those minutes, lose myself to my book, relax, and enjoy the quiet. Was I crazy? The first week I thought so.

The rules were given. Take enough reading material to occupy 15 minutes. Do not get up. Do not ask anyone, including me, a question. Just read. The first week, a few students tried to test my rules. I had to teacher-frown and finger-point them back to their seats. A few tried to sleep. One or two brave ones came to ask me about an unknown word. I had to repeat the frown, put a finger to my lips, and motion students back to their seats.

After those first days of testing my resolve and deciding I was serious about this quiet reading time, things settled down. Unbelievable. Every so often, just for reassurance, I glanced up out of the corner of my eye at my very calm class. It was not always completely quiet. Occasionally I'd hear someone softly reading, but it was so quiet that I heard a teacher remark in the hall to her class as she passed my door, "They're all reading in there." The

timer beeped, and we knew our 15 minutes of SSR were finished.
What next? There's more to my madness.

At first, when the timer beeped, students ran, full speed
ahead, to the corner rug where I was reading my novel. As they
charged, legs and arms spilling and stepping everywhere, getting
the perfect seat, I knew we had to restore some order to the
mayhem. Translated for the children, this meant "wait your turn
and walk." After a few days, I noticed some of them didn't close
their books when the timer rang. Now that there was no rush to the
rug, they could steal a few more seconds and read a little further.

I don't know what they expected when they arrived on the
rug, but I'm sure it wasn't what they got. I held up the book I'd
been reading, told them the title, and shared a little about what was
happening. They looked bug-eyed at me, as if to say, "What is she
doing?" Then I asked if any of them wanted to tell us a little about
what they were reading? A few hands went up tentatively that first
day, but as we all listened and students began to enjoy having an
audience, the volunteers grew in number daily. We heard about the
exploits of Junie B. Jones in the series by Barbara Park, the
mysteries and adventures involving the Magic Tree House in the
series by Mary Pope Osborne, and the scary scenes in the
Goosebumps series by R.L. Stine. We also looked at picture books.
What surprised me was students' eagerness to hear about my book.
Someone always asked, "Aren't you going to tell us what's
happening in your book?"

I soon discovered that I couldn't always share with students
what was happening in my book. Some topics just didn't seem
appropriate for third-grade ears. I thought about
other elements of a book that we might share
besides the story line and decided to try
sharing emotions and feelings. My novel, I
explained, was good but very sad. Did they ever
read anything that made them feel sad? I was
doubtful that they had, considering what they
read, but one of my girls surprised me and shot her hand into the
air. "I know just what you mean," she empathized. "Listen to this."
She rummaged in her desk for a minute and pulled out *Johnny*

> What surprised me
> was students'
> eagerness to hear
> about my book.

Appleseed by Steven Kellogg (1988). She turned to a page near the beginning and proceeded to read about the death of Johnny's mother and baby brother, all of which took place before his second birthday. Then before anyone had a chance to speak, she flipped to the back of the book and exclaimed, "And that's not all. Listen." She read to us about Johnny and his healthy life and how, when he was older, sickness came over him and he eventually died. There was silence. After remembering to breathe, I thought out loud about how amazing it was that words on a page could make us feel so many different emotions. We started talking about stories that made us feel good and even laugh out loud. We giggled over a few poems from *A Light in the Attic* (Silverstein, 1981) and laughed about Junie B. and Handsome Warren (Park, 1996). I was beginning to think anything might have been possible.

I love the characters in books and often enjoy a good character study as much as the action. I wondered if we could share our characters and talk about their traits. I eased students into this idea by telling them a little about Johnnie Mae from *River, Cross My Heart* (Clarke, 1999). She was definitely a girl who could take care of herself. After Johnnie's younger sister, Clara, was insulted by a bully named Bessie, Johnnie knew she had to defend Clara. I read a paragraph out loud that includes the scene in which Bessie's nose spills blood and mucus after being punched by Johnnie Mae. I chose to read this portion of the book because it shows a realistic fight between two kids. When I finished reading, my students cheered.

Several days later, as we continued talking about our characters, an argument erupted between two students who had read the same Magic Tree House book. Jack and Annie, the main characters, had all sorts of adventures. Samantha, who was telling us about the book, was describing Annie as a fearless adventurer. As an aside, she mentioned Jack, who is always scared of everything. No sooner were the words out of her mouth when Jarrett, who also had read the book, jumped in to defend the spineless character of Jack. "It isn't that he is scared," he exclaimed. "He likes to read and study things, that's all. And he wears glasses."

"What is it about the characters of Jack and Annie that make him appear cowardly and her full of adventure and extremely brave?" I asked. "Is everybody in agreement that she is the brave one?" They were definitely not. The questions elicited an entire range of responses. Some children felt that the author tells us who is brave and who isn't, like reading a menu. The majority of students generally dismissed this idea. Those children who had read more extensively argued with vehemence that it just wasn't so. Authors do not always tell us in so many words that Annie is brave and Jack is not. It is up to the reader to figure it out.

"But how?" I asked. That is when the books were pulled out and paragraphs read. Bravery was definitely illustrated for Annie, but Jack remained in the gray area. Some felt he, too, was brave; others saw "scaredy-cat" tendencies in him. At that point, I had to ask, "What does this tell you about books?" More than a few hands went up, and the unified response was that we don't all get the same thing out of books.

As book sharing continued daily, I worried—what next? I tried to give our exploration a sense of direction. Our basal reading series introduced the concept of first- and third-person in third grade. So I offered the question, "Who is telling your story, and how do you know?" After a bit of a struggle understanding this idea, the students seemed to enjoy reading paragraphs and supporting their beliefs about who was telling the story. The amazing part was that they listened to and challenged one another. One boy claimed, "Joe was telling the story," but then went on to read that Joe did this or Joe said that. Indignant voices cried out, "That can't be right. Joe isn't telling the story. He wouldn't say his own name!" Before long, I noticed that more and more children were bringing their books with them to the rug, just in case. Backing up their statements with text seemed to be gaining popularity. "This character, Mark, he's rude and lazy," Josh stated, frantically flipping pages. "I can't find it; just come back to me," and so on we went to another. Later, I saw a hand waving wildly out of the corner of my eye. It's Josh and he's ready: "This is the part I wanted to read:

> The amazing part was that [the students] listened to and challenged one another.

'Mark shoved his book bag at his friend to carry.' See, the bag is heavy, and he doesn't even ask. He just shoves it at him."

I took another chance in this exploration of wanting to blend in, becoming less teacher and more reader. We formulated a question of the day together, and one person volunteered to be our leader. I sat back, listened, and contributed when called on. Was I relaxed? Of course not, but I thought it might be possible when I looked around at the expectant faces, eagerly focused not on me but on a little third-grade girl. And then I heard her clear, childlike voice ask, "Who wants to share?"

LITERATURE CITED

Clarke, B. (1999). *River, cross my heart*. Boston: Little, Brown.

Kellogg, S. (1988). *Johnny Appleseed*. New York: Morrow Junior Books.

Lamb, W. (1998). *I know this much is true*. New York: Regan Books.

Osborne, M.P. (2001). *Magic tree house boxed set (Vols. 1–4)*. New York: Random House.

Park, B. (1996). *Junie B. Jones loves Handsome Warren*. New York: Random House.

Silverstein, S. (1981). *A light in the attic*. New York: Harper & Row.

Stine, R.L. (1993). *Goosebumps (Books 1–4)*. New York: Scholastic.

—Jennifer Olson—
TEACHER EDUCATOR

Jennifer has been a classroom teacher in Baltimore County, Maryland, and in Williamsburg, Virginia. She spent five years in each district, and all her years were with second- or third-grade students. Now, she is a graduate student who works with preservice teachers in the Elementary Education Program at the University of Georgia.

Jennifer jumped on the chance to take a seminar that would allow her to read whatever she chose. She thought that freedom would be a good way to break into being a full-time graduate student slowly. What she learned about herself as a reader and as a developing teacher educator surprised her. The seminar discussions brought her right back to what had always been important to her as a reader—talking about what she read.

Jennifer's favorite reading from the Readers as Teachers and Teachers as Readers seminar was TAKING LOTTIE HOME by Terry Kay (2000) because she has always enjoyed Kay's writing, and she continues to be interested in reading books by local authors. Kay is an author from Athens, Georgia, whose appearance at a local library prompted Jennifer to pick more than one of his books for reading, and TAKING LOTTIE HOME was his most recent book at the time.

CHAPTER 6

Full Circle
Jennifer Olson

t is our family ritual—bath, books, bed, in that order. As
Livia and I snuggle up, ready for our nightly reading, my
mind runs through the list of things I need to read for
graduate school, but quickly the comfort of her bed and her warm
toes bring me back to reality. For the moment, I enjoy being with
my daughter as we share books, laughs, words, and stories. Tonight
we read *If You Give a Pig a Pancake* by Laura Numeroff (1998).
The book is one of my favorites for its predictable nature and
because Livia can join in the reading; she is only 3. On a night that
a long list of articles to read for graduate school is not far from my
mind, I am glad for her choice. As I listen to my own voice and as
Livia's voice chimes in, I think about how my own reading life has
come full circle.

During class time for the seminar, facilitator Michelle
Commeyras always allowed time for us participants to write about
our reading and how it enhances our teaching lives. Fresh in my
mind at one seminar meeting were Livia's warm toes and the
rhythm of *If You Give a Pig a Pancake*. I made a connection
between the circular nature of the book and my own reading life,
regarding how simply being given the chance to read and being
given time and permission to follow my own reading wishes
brought me back to where I had been before I tried to force my
reading habits in another direction. I wrote the following poem:

Full Circle

If you give a teacher a book…

Chances are she will find a person to share it with.

If she finds a person to share it with…

She may even join a book group…

Or take a college course.

Chances are she will make some connections
to her own life...

So she'll want to explore those connections...

She may even study teaching
and what it means to teach teachers.

She may even become a doctoral graduate student...

And begin to explore her own subjectivities...

Or try to frame a research question.

What is it that she wants to learn about?

Chances are she will read many journals
and research articles...

Trying to find her theoretical framework

Trying to find her place in the big picture
of teacher education.

When she talks about teaching she gets excited...

And wants to talk about what it means to her...

Chances are she will take many classes
on teaching and learning.

She may even find some on teaching reading...

Or on teaching learners to be readers...

And why teaching students to be learners is so important.

And somewhere along the way...

She will remember that reading is a key to learning.

And someone will recommend a book they just read...

And chances are that if you give a teacher a book...

She'll start reading again.

I enrolled in the Readers as Teachers and Teachers as Readers seminar to explore other teachers' reading. I ended up discovering more about myself as a reader. While reading *If You Give a Pig a Pancake* to my daughter, I realized that I had come full circle. I wonder about how easy it was to lose touch with myself as a reader. As I looked back on my own reading history, I realized how I had lost my reader self, and this seminar helped me find it again. Terry Kay's words in *Taking Lottie Home* (2000) brought home to me how I couldn't walk away from something as important as reading: "Son, once you been somewhere, you don't never leave it out of sight behind you, you just drag it along with you, like a cranky old dog on a leash" (p. 215).

As I remember my childhood, reading was part of my life. When we were kids, my sister made up a game called Monkey. The rules were simple. It could involve two or more players, but she always was the big monkey and everyone else was a little monkey. In the game, the little monkeys bothered the big monkey when the big monkey was reading. The game ended when the big monkey said, "Go away, I am reading."

I wonder about how easy it was to lose touch with myself as a reader.

My sister devised this game as a way to keep me from bothering her when she was reading! As a child, she always was reading, and I always wanted her to play with me. I was somewhat jealous of her ability to lose herself in her book so much that she did not even want to play. I did not understand that. I enjoyed reading, but I think what I enjoyed more about reading was the sense of accomplishment that came with checking a book off my list or putting it in my done pile. There is a difference to me. She was reading because she was absorbed in the story, and I was reading because I wanted to say I had read something.

I was always a good reader in elementary school. I got good grades and enjoyed reading class. My fourth-grade teacher was the first teacher that challenged me with reading. She required us to keep a reading log, so I carefully kept track of every book I read. The first time I turned it in, I was so proud. I had the longest list of books of anyone in the class. When the teacher returned the reading log, her comment said she was unable to tell if I had really read the book. I did not understand her comment, so after school I asked her about it. I told her that I had indeed read the books on my list. She said she knew I had read the words, but that I had not told her anything about what I had read. I think that was when I began to understand more about reading. Reading was more than just the words in books. Reading was about *me* and words and books.

My models for reading as a youth were my parents and my sister. My sister would read anything she could get her hands on: Harlequin romances, or books by J.R.R. Tolkien, Isaac Asimov, and Stephen King. She had multiple books, each bookmarked where she left off reading. Just as I never understood my sister's reading, I didn't understand my parents', either. They read incessantly. They both liked Jane Austen and Georgette Heyer, and my mother liked Phyllis Whitney. But they read books over and over again. I never understood that. I still don't reread books very often, but I have done it a few times and been glad I did. I reread *Catch-22* by Joseph Heller (1955) as an adult and discovered things I had never understood as a teenager. I reread *Their Eyes Were Watching God* by Zora Neale Hurston (1978) and was awed by the language she used.

After reading Anne McCrary Sullivan's 1991 article about "schools separating students from the pleasure of reading" (p. 40), I can see where I experienced some of the same things as a young reader. My reading life in school was quite different from my reading life at home. My summers and vacations were quite full of reading; we had no television when I was growing up. I depended on losing myself in those stories. It was my imaginative entertainment.

At school, my reading was different. I remember the first time I was required to write a paper on something that I had read in school. It was seventh grade, when I still thought essay was spelled *SA* (as if there was some code behind the letters *S* and *A*). The book that I had read was *Black Boy* by Richard Wright (1945). I remember really liking the characters and enjoying reading the book, but my teacher did not like my essay on the book. Similar to my fourth-grade teacher, she was expecting more than a "superficial" response. Reading in school then became a burden. I was supposed to search for something beyond the story and my reaction to it, but no one would tell me what that was. So I read at home without telling, without sharing. This hidden reading life stayed with me until college, even through college. I was scared of all the literature classes, yet I was drawn to reading books that were valued by others. I never did find all the metaphors and symbols in T.S. Eliot's poetry. I never did understand exactly what the "Buried

Child" is in Sam Shepard's 1971 play. But I did enjoy reading both Eliot's poetry and Shepherd's play.

Since finishing college, I have openly immersed myself in books. I read trashy novels, suspense novels, and even some nonfiction. A week at the beach is seven books for me—a book a day. While I was a public school teacher, summers off from school meant I was free to read again—no papers to grade and no lesson plans to write. Sometimes I would read through my classroom library, sometimes I would go to the library and pick a book because of the book jacket, and sometimes I would go to a bookstore and pick a new novel. Now I depend heavily on peer recommendations, but occasionally I indulge in a spontaneous purchase of a book that sparked some spur-of-the-moment interest.

This hidden reading life stayed with me until college, even through college.

One day, the reading specialist at my school encouraged me to join a teacher book group at our school. The incentive was free books. You see, I really did like books, and who could turn down free books? I thought that we would be discussing children's literature in light of how we could use the books in our own classrooms. To my delight and surprise, we just talked. Here were teachers that I admired, talking about books and what they meant to them personally, not what the books meant to them professionally. We did not read to find some symbolism or hidden theme. We read to find our own meaning. I still remember every book we read: *Shiloh* (Naylor, 1991), *Lyddie* (Paterson, 1991), *The Big Book of Peace* (Durrell & Sachs, 1990), and *The Place My Words Are Looking For* (Janeczka, 1990). The fact that I can remember the title of each book without looking on a shelf lets me know what value I placed on that teachers' reading group.

When I moved to Athens, Georgia, a lot changed in my life. I was no longer a teacher but a full-time mother of two. I obviously missed the day-to-day challenge of teaching. I found my way into a neighborhood book club. What did we do? We chose books we wanted to share with others, and then we talked about them. Through the book club, I was exposed to some southern authors such as Terry Kay and his amazing book *To Dance With a White*

Dog (1991). We all laughed over Rick Bragg's stories in *All Over But the Shoutin'* (1998). I read historical novels such as *Gone to Soldiers* by Marge Piercy (1987). We also ventured into the mind of Richard Feynman in *"Surely You're Joking Mister Feynman": Adventures of a Curious Character* (1997). I know I would not have chosen to read the Feynman book on my own. The group made a difference. We read aloud sections, we discussed characters, and we shared our own reactions to the book.

Now, as a graduate assistant in the Elementary Education Program at the University of Georgia, I hear many of the preservice teachers' conversations about teaching reading. They are scared of exactly how to teach reading, and they are worried about balancing whole language and phonics. Yet the preservice teachers crave discussions about using children's literature in their classrooms. I began to see that one of my roles as a teacher educator is to allow those discussions in my college classroom. I think somewhere in the back of my mind I was hoping and wishing that the preservice teachers would remember this sharing of ideas and note how important the discussions were to their own learning. Maybe they would incorporate the same kinds of discussions into their own classrooms one day.

As a student myself, I have felt the tension between what I want to read and what I should read. My life has become more academic since beginning graduate school, and I feel my reading should follow suit. I still have the same features of who I am, but now the leisure time is gone. I feel the constraints of being pulled in many directions, so how can I make time to find a theme in my books and reading? Are these the same tensions other teachers feel in the classroom or the same tensions preservice teachers feel as they learn about teaching? I have found myself wondering how I can help my aspiring teachers hang on to their own reading lives.

> *I have found myself wondering how I can help my aspiring teachers hang on to their own reading lives.*

Imagine my surprise as I walked into room 319 on August 21, 2001, for READ 9010: Readers as Teachers and Teachers as Readers. We wrote quotes on the whiteboard, we talked, we discussed, we listened, and we shared what we had been reading. One of the quotes that I wrote on the board was, "Do you ever let your mind wander, or do you always steer it? I find steering more productive. Well, I recommend a good wander" (Malarkey, 2000, p. 266). The quote was from one of the first books I read as I allowed myself to read for me again. I allowed myself to wander. So now, I still walk the balance between academic reading and personal reading. But each day, I try to find a place for reading for me. Within that time are the release, solitude, escape, and entertainment I know I need.

This is my journey. As I travel the road of graduate student, mother, and educator, I read and I still want to put myself into the words I read. You see, now I feel that I belong with those words and books. I need to keep that connection. As I teach future educators, I want them also to see how reading connects to their lives and mine.

REFERENCES

Sullivan, A. (1991). The natural reading life: A high-school anomaly. *English Journal, 80,* 40–46.

LITERATURE CITED

Bragg, R. (1998). *All over but the shoutin'.* New York: Vintage Books.
Durrell, A., & Sachs, M. (Eds.) (1990). *The big book of peace.* New York: Dutton.
Feynman, R. (1997). *"Surely you're joking Mister Feynman": Adventures of a curious character.* New York: W.W. Norton.
Heller, J. (1955). *Catch-22.* New York: Dell.
Hurston, Z.N. (1978). *Their eyes were watching God.* Urbana, IL: Illini Books.
Janeczka, P. (1990). *The place my words are looking for.* New York: Bradbury Press.
Kay, T. (1991). *To dance with a white dog.* New York: Washington Square Press.
Kay, T. (2000). *Taking Lottie home.* New York: HarperCollins.
Malarkey, T. (2000). *An obvious enchantment.* New York: Random House.
Naylor, P. (1991). *Shiloh.* New York: Atheneum.
Numeroff, L. (1998). *If you give a pig a pancake.* New York: HarperCollins.
Paterson, K. (1991). *Lyddie.* New York: Lodestar.
Piercy, M. (1987). *Gone to soldiers.* New York: Fawcett Crest.
Shephard, S. (1971). Buried child. In *Seven plays* (pp. 61–132). Toronto: Bantam Books.
Wright, R. (1945). *Black boy.* New York: Harper & Brothers.

—Renèe Tootle—
PREKINDERGARTEN TEACHER

Renèe has taught prekindergarten for six years. She has worked in both a prekindergarten Head Start center and in an elementary school.

Renèe was thrilled to have the option of taking a course that allowed her to read anything that she chose. She has always loved to read and was eager to be able to choose her own reading for coursework. Although hesitant at first, Renèe learned about herself, her own reading habits, and how her own reading affects even her prekindergarten classroom.

Renèe's favorite reading from the Readers as Teachers and Teachers as Readers seminar was MAMA MAKES UP HER MIND: AND OTHER DANGERS OF SOUTHERN LIVING by Bailey White (1993) because the stories made her laugh. She could see herself in many of the situations the author describes.

CHAPTER 7

My Reading Choices Soothe Me

Renèe Tootle

can't remember a time that reading wasn't part of my life. My mom read to me as a young child, and then I began reading on my own. I haven't stopped. I chose to take part in the Readers as Teachers and Teachers as Readers seminar because I wanted to learn how I could bring my love of reading into the classroom. Our first assignment was to read for at least 20 minutes each day. I shivered with excitement. Someone, a professor, was telling me to read anything I wanted every day. It seemed too simple. If I got so excited about the permission to read, then possibly children would as well. Now this idea was easy for my prekindergarten students and me. They already were begging their moms and dads to read to them every night. But what about the stories I heard from other teachers? Did their students respond well to the chance to read books of their choice? Each week, I came to the seminar eager to hear about other teachers' experiences. I also looked forward to hearing how they spent their 20 minutes of reading each day. Unfortunately, I hit a snag.

It seemed as if everyone was reading books that had some significant personal meaning or were somehow educational. I, on the other hand, was choosing to read my favorite romances, historical fiction, magazines, and newspapers. These readings brought me pleasure, but I didn't feel confident that others would be interested. I felt that what I was reading wasn't good enough. Now don't get me wrong; the people in my class were caring and supportive, but in my mind, I felt inadequate. This made me think about young readers. What if they experience the same insecurities that I felt? A struggling reader may be embarrassed by the types of books that she reads, just as I was. Maybe a strong reader is interested in a particular series or genre unfamiliar to her peers. I realized that no matter what reading ability a child has, there might be a time when she feels uncertain about a reading choice. I realized that as a teacher, it is my job to introduce students to many types of literature and provide a time when children can voluntarily share what it is that they are reading. There are also times when students need to read what the teacher has decided is educationally valuable. Most of all, I hope to teach my students that people read for different reasons. I happen to read mostly for pleasure, and after trying other choices for my reading time, I finally made peace with the idea that my reading choices are fine because of the joy I get from them.

The next challenge I faced was finding ways to share my reading life with my students. I had a very difficult time with this because of their age. The things that I read were not appropriate to share with my 4-year-old students. So, I started simple. Several times a week during silent reading time, I would bring in my book from home and read it. I felt that even if I couldn't share the contents of my story, I could show them that I enjoyed reading by modeling reading for them. I once heard a first grader say that he knew his teacher liked to read because "she reads books that she doesn't even have to." I thought about how much that teacher must have taught her students by modeling such behavior. She probably didn't even realize the impact her actions had on her young readers. It would have been so easy for her to be doing something else during her students' silent reading time. My students never commented on my book or asked what I was reading, but I felt I was affecting their reading attitudes in some positive way. I also shared my reading life with my students by telling them how much I love to read. I told them about my favorite times to read and how it made me feel. I love to snuggle under the covers at night and escape into a character's life. During this time, I am able to wind down from my busy day. I try to share with students children's books that mean something to me. If a

> A struggling reader may be embarrassed by the types of books that she reads, just as I was.

book makes me cry like Shel Silverstein's (1986) *The Giving Tree* or gives me the giggles like Barbara Park's (2001) Junie B. Jones series, I don't try to hide it. I talk with my students about my feelings.

During the Readers as Teachers and Teachers as Readers seminar, I was asked to think about how my reading made a difference in my life. This was hard at first because reading is such a normal part of my life that I really hadn't thought about it much. I guess the biggest impact reading has on my life both personally and professionally is the way it soothes me. I can have the most stressful day at work and be ready to cry when I get home, but if I can take a few minutes to read, I tend to calm down. Reading allows me to take a mini mental vacation from all of life's pressures and problems. After reading a good book by one of my favorite authors—Sandra Brown, Karen Robards, or Catherine Coulter—I can go back into the classroom refreshed and ready to tackle teaching again. The most recent example of this was the September 11, 2001, tragedy in New York City, Washington, D.C., and western Pennsylvania. That was one of the most stressful and frightening days that I had ever experienced. The uncertainty and lack of information had me longing for the chance to go home and read a newspaper or watch the news to gather information. Even though I was reading about tragic events, I was calmed by the fact that I was no longer in the dark about the events that transpired that day. I devoured every piece of information like a starving animal. I was glued to the Internet and television. As I became numb from all the frightening details, I soon longed for the escape of a new intrigue or romance. Soon I sank into a new story. I don't even remember what book it was, but just for a little while I was able to get away from the horror that had occurred.

This reminded me that if I could be calmed and soothed by a story, then probably my students could as well. I can recall many times when a funny story brought a huge smile to a face that had previously been solemn. Stories have a way of connecting with students in ways that they may not have ever previously connected with reading. Maybe they lost a loved one, or their parents are having problems. Maybe they are having trouble with a friend or are lacking self-confidence. Good stories often let these children know that others understand their feelings. Sometimes, stories give children the confidence to talk about their problems, allowing them to start to heal.

I learned a great deal about myself during my reading journey in the seminar. The most important idea I have taken away from this experience is to encourage reading every day. Through conversations with children of all ages, I think I am beginning to get the big picture. Children like to be read to. It doesn't matter their age. Just the simple act of reading to your students and in front of them does wonders for their attitudes about reading. Other children in my school mentioned that they enjoyed getting book suggestions from their teachers. So, teachers, share your ideas with your students! Many are listening. And listen to your students when they are eager to share a book. I have a student who seems to get great joy from sharing books with me during free playtime. She often takes my hand and leads me to my rocking chair. She sits me down, pulls up the small rocking chair, and reads her favorite books to me. Her enthusiasm for sharing books is rubbing off on others in the class. I now see other students reading and sharing with one another. Many like to pretend to be the teacher and read to the "students." I hope this positive reading attitude will follow these children into the years to come.

Children like to be read to. It doesn't matter their age.

I come away from this journey with the drive to share more of my reading life with my students in any way that I can. I have found the confidence to be proud of my reading choices and the desire to occasionally broaden my reading horizon. I will never know what reading pleasure awaits me unless I choose to reach out and find it. I would never have read the anecdotes of Bailey White (1993) if I had not taken the baby step to read something different. This journey has been good for me.

LITERATURE CITED

Park, B. (2001). *Junie B. Jones collection (Books 1–4)*. New York: Random House.

Silverstein, S. (1986). *The giving tree*. New York: HarperCollins.

White, B. (1993). *Mama makes up her mind: And other dangers of southern living*. New York: Vintage Books.

—Aimee Castleman—
EARLY INTERVENTION PROGRAM TEACHER

Aimee began teaching prekindergarten and did that for two years. She is now an early intervention program teacher at West Jackson Primary School in Winder, Georgia.

Aimee's favorite reading from the Readers as Teachers and Teachers as Readers seminar was GIRL WITH A PEARL EARRING (Chevalier, 1999). She loves historical fiction and a good story, and this book is both.

CHAPTER 8

All You Have to Do Is Listen and Enjoy
Aimee Castleman

Hello. My name is Aimee, and I am a bookaholic. No, I don't need caffeine, or nicotine, or alcohol, or any other chemical substance to get me through the day; all I need is a good book. Sometimes the need is so strong that I will let other important things go by the wayside just so I can get that fix. It wouldn't matter that my house is a wreck or that someone just drowned in a pile of my dirty laundry. No, if I'm reading a good book, I wouldn't even notice. When there is a book in my hands, I become THE BOOK. The scenes play out in my head like a movie. I become so engrossed that I won't even hear my husband trying to talk to me; instead, I hear the characters speaking and other sounds described in the book. I feel so many emotions while reading a good book—sadness, joy, pain, hurt, fear, anger, and excitement. Excitement is my favorite! I got so excited while reading *Harry Potter and the Sorcerer's Stone* (Rowling, 1997) that I actually had to put my hand over the bottom of the page so my eyes wouldn't stray and give something away. I just love that feeling! Wouldn't it be wonderful if our students felt this way about reading? I would like nothing more than to give the gift of a wonderful book experience to my students and let them be swept away.

There are many wonderful young readers out there who become so involved in their readings and who love reading. I was one of those young readers. I read all the time—short books, long books, fiction and nonfiction books, picture books, magazines, basically whatever I

> *I would like nothing more than to give the gift of a wonderful book experience to my students and let them be swept away.*

could get my hands on. I wasn't trying to be the class winner of most books read; I didn't need or want points for reading. I just loved reading. So I read.

Some of my best childhood memories come from reading favorite books. My grandma had the Laura Ingalls Wilder books (1953) at her house, and I remember reading and sharing those books with her. What a great book experience that was for me. I cannot imagine how my life would have been or would be now without loving to read. So working with students who would rather be doing anything else other than reading has been a challenge for me.

As an early intervention reading teacher, I work with the students who don't want to read because they struggle with it. They stumble along in that word-by-painful-word phase, but amazingly enough they understand what they read. I believe that they really want to enjoy books but feel trapped by what they can read.

Each day, my students are supposed to bring a book of their choice to read to me during our time together. They tended to choose those easy, no-plot, controlled vocabulary books that are usually incredibly boring. (And I wonder why they aren't enjoying books?) One by one, they brought their books over to read to me: One by one, I endured that monotonous reading voice. Not one of them smiled at any point in the book, not even at the one funny part! I asked, "Well, what did you think? Did you like it?" Every single one of them said, "Yeah. I liked it." I was not convinced. The worst part is that, even though they were reading easy books, they were still stumbling on the words. And what's worse than a monotonous stumbler? I know it is my job as a teacher to help students become fluent readers; however, as a self-proclaimed lover of reading, it is also my responsibility to help students find joy in reading. I believe that both can be accomplished.

My school does that read-and-test-for-points routine, but thankfully, our students are not discouraged to check out books that are not on their level. I wanted to encourage my students to step out of the easy-book box. Because they would not bring any fun and challenging books to me, I decided to bring the books to them. I chose several books as possible read-alouds and presented them to the group one day. Students looked over the books, and I read the back of each one to give them some idea as to what the book was about. Then we took a vote. It was unanimous: *The Stories Julian Tells* by Ann Cameron (1989) was to be the book. Unfortunately, our time together ended that day, so I told them we would begin the book the next day. Honestly, they did not look too excited about it, but I was determined to show them the fun that could be found in reading.

The next day, toward the end of our time, I picked up the book. I held it up and said, "All you have to do is listen and enjoy." Some of them were finishing up something else, and they looked up at me with these "Yeah, whatever, lady" faces and then went right back to work. What happened next was wonderful. All the students who were doing something else had literally dropped their pencils and were smiling up at me by the time I reached the bottom of page 2 of the story. One boy even got out of his seat to come and stand over my shoulder to read along with me. After finishing the first story, I heard a lovely chorus of, "Read another one, please!" Students laughed throughout the other stories in the book and were so excited to hear more of them. Finally, the day came when we finished the book. When I asked what they thought of it, students could hardly contain themselves:

"Wow! Mrs. Castleman, that was really great!"

"I liked when the dad told them about frogs in their shoes!"

"Can you read that again?"

What a nice change these reactions were from the ones of boredom I'd previously gotten from my students.

We have continued to read some wonderful books together. It is really starting to rub off; students are bringing good books to class to read to me that are challenging and interesting. Several days ago, the boy who had stood over my shoulder brought a great book to me. It was sort of a spooky book that his teacher had out around Halloween. It was a difficult book, but he read it beautifully. He didn't stumble, and he read with expression! And at one point in the book, he laughed and said, "That was so funny."

> [S]tudents are bringing good books to class to read to me that are challenging and interesting.

LITERATURE CITED

Cameron, A. (1989). *The stories Julian tells*. New York: Random House.

Chevalier, T. (1999). *Girl with a pearl earring*. New York: Dutton.

Rowling, J.K. (1997). *Harry Potter and the sorcerer's stone*. New York: Scholastic.

Wilder, L.I. (1953). *Little house on the prairie*. New York: HarperTrophy.

—Sharon Dowling Cox—
SPEECH-LANGUAGE PATHOLOGIST

Sharon has been a speech-language pathologist for the past 20 years. She has worked in a variety of settings, including 6 years in a preschool psychoeducational center and 14 years in public schools. She has had shorter-term experiences in several private-practice settings, including a hospital and rehabilitative facilities. She was employed in her present position as an elementary school speech-language pathologist for 8 years before taking an educational leave of absence to complete a specialist's degree in reading education.

Sharon's favorite reading from the Readers as Teachers and Teachers as Readers seminar was BEFORE WOMEN HAD WINGS by Connie May Fowler (1996) because the author tells her story so poignantly that Sharon stayed up all night reading the book and felt like a kid again.

CHAPTER 9

Dissolving Boundaries Through Language, Literacy, and Learning
Sharon Dowling Cox

The Reciprocal Sharing of Reading Lives

"Mrs. Cox, did you have to learn new vocabulary words when you went back to school?" I paused momentarily, and the word *pedagogy* came to mind. Tina, a fifth-grade student, asked this question during a language lesson with one of her peers. We were discussing strategies that could be used when taking vocabulary tests and using what we already know about words to highlight the importance of making meaning from what we read. As I reflected with these two students on the experience of my reentry into graduate school, I shared feelings of my initial resistance at having to embrace the new word *pedagogy*. More words popped into mind as I related strategies I used when I encountered difficult text and found writing styles in journal articles and scholarly texts to be challenging. When I confessed that I often used the dictionary to look up unknown words to better understand what I read, both students stared at me transfixed. This genuine conversation gave new meaning to my prior efforts to explicitly teach new vocabulary. My students were helping me connect my learning with theirs. At this point, I began to feel as though the new words came unexpectedly, like the wind swirling softly into our conversations. As if propelled by breezes, these words moved our thoughts, feelings, and experiences, settling around us as new understandings were revealed.

When I began to share my personal reading life with my students, I did not realize the powerful shift that had begun as my pedagogy took on new meaning. I knew that merging the disciplines of reading and speech-language pathology was a new way for me to teach to the broad curriculum objectives designed to help students become more fluent in oral expression while fostering competence in language comprehension. However, I was learning that talking about books offered a more natural and practical forum for fostering overall language development, as compared to looking at pictures from a worksheet, which seemed a contrived way of teaching and learning.

As a reader who teaches, I am now engaged in the process of targeting speech and language goals that have been established in the students' individualized educational plans (IEPs), while integrating my reading and readings from teacher- and student-chosen texts with our communicative interactions.

I find the flow of instruction speckled with unexpected questions or comments from both students and myself. Their comments often surprise me. I feel privileged to learn from their honesty and ingenuity:

"This book is not really interesting yet."

"I visualize how the person in the story looks."

"She (Anne Sullivan) reminds me of Louis Braille because they both had to leave their parents."

"An adjective shows strong and intense feeling."

Boundaries were dissolving. Whenever I share myself as a reader, I engage with students more as individuals with whom I share an ageless common bond—we are all readers. The traditional roles of teacher/speech-language pathologist as giver of knowledge and the student as receiver seem to be dissolving along with the endless copying and paper shuffling of worksheets on my part. There is more spontaneous laughter and expressions of satisfaction as students make connections between school learning experiences and the reality of their lives outside of school. Words have created these moments, fashioning

I find the flow of instruction speckled with unexpected questions or comments from both students and myself.

an atmosphere of excitement and openness. This spontaneous shift in the direction of our words invites students into a dialogue of sharing and thinking that values their comments and questions as serious contributions to our learning process.

"Tell us about a book you're reading," asked a student during an articulation lesson. She and one of her peers had just told me about a book they had read while working on goals to establish carryover of /s/ and /z/ sounds in their conversational speech. A smile graced my face as I said, "Did I ever tell you about the book that I stayed up all night reading that made me cry?" Just two weeks before, I had finished reading *Before Women Had Wings* by Connie May Fowler (1996). The words from that story were still tickling my thoughts, causing me to relive memories of this book at a moment's notice.

As I shared with the students the emotional connections I felt with the main character, Bird, whose given name is Avocet Abigail Jackson, the memories began to unfold. Avocet and her sister are both named after birds by their mother who uses the logic that if they are named after something with wings, maybe they will be able to fly above the adversity in their lives. I expressed my fascination with the author's skill in using words to create a powerful story that kept me glued to the pages hour after hour. I revisited the range of emotions that surfaced during my reading experience and my sadness at having the book end. Thanks to a student's question, my passion for reading was once again revealed as the winds of words created these moments.

Relaxed yet structured, casual yet professional, and enjoyable yet serious—this is how I now define the learning relationships I develop with students. It is as though my own reading experiences have allowed me to become more in touch with my emotions. While talking about my experiences as a reader, both intellectual and emotional doors have opened that allow my students to know me. They, in turn, seem to be sharing more of themselves with me.

With my invitation, students share what books they read make them think and feel. Our conversations prompt them to share their reasons for reading and rereading and how and why they choose certain books. Some students tell me that they take their books with them on road trips but may forget to read them, and others tell me that they read for extended periods of time without being told to by their parents.

When I began to know the students in my speech and language therapy program as readers, I felt that it was important to know what they read so I could make recommendations to help them expand their reading lives and ways of thinking about reading. As I read children's books—the class anthologies and trade and library books that students read—I thought of the types of literature I could talk about. Clearly, I could talk with students about the children's literature I read, but what about my adult reading? When I read *Remembering Blue* (2000), my next Connie May Fowler selection, I told my students who struggled in both reading and language how the speed of my reading changed. I explained how there were times when I read slower to visualize the descriptive scenes presented by the writer and how I read faster with anticipation when I wanted to know what would happen next.

Once, when I talked with two fifth-grade students about a book they were reading for class—*The Kid in the Red Jacket* by Barbara Park (1987)—I chose to read aloud my favorite descriptive phrases because they so aptly described how "the kid" felt about moving. The descriptions were in part why I enjoyed the story. The feelings seemed so real and honest for someone in that situation. Although the students agreed that this book was a good one, I was deeply disappointed when I found out that this particular group of fifth-grade students did not choose to read the book for enjoyment. Instead, their purpose for reading was the number of Accelerated Reader points they could gain. Accelerated Reader is a computer-assisted assessment of students' comprehension of books in which the student takes a multiple-choice comprehension test on the content of a book he or she has read, earning points based on his or her results. These students' revelation, along with the fact they would not be able to have a discussion with their peers about the book because of lack of time in the classroom schedule, furthered my own intention to be a living, breathing teacher-reader who talks about books.

Discussing what we read offers invaluable opportunities to gain students' perspectives on their lives and learning. Communicating about literature as an integral part of instruction has allowed me to move outside traditional boundaries in my teaching practices. Talking to students about books allows me to see and interact with them as individuals, according to their particular needs. Let the words continue!

> *Discussing what we read offers invaluable opportunities to gain students' perspectives on their lives and learning.*

The Genesis of a Book Club: Reading to Lead

I struggled with my desire to start a book club. How would I fit something new into an already overloaded schedule as a speech-language pathologist? I brought the idea to the Readers as Teachers and Teachers as Readers seminar. Many of the teachers had experience with book clubs and literature circles. "Start small and build from there," several advised. "Focus on making it fun, and stay away from an academic atmosphere," they all agreed.

Casting all caution and lingering uncertainties aside, my passion prevailed, and one Friday morning I broached the subject with my principal. He offered me his full support and asked for a brief proposal to review. After reading the proposal, he suggested that I take my idea to the staff members. They gave a round of applause when I shared my idea of inviting third-grade students to meet once a week over breakfast to talk about their reading. The following dialogue gives a sampling of some questions from my colleagues and my answers:

Q: Will they have to read the same book?

A: No, they may choose to read and share whatever books they would like.

Q: You do expect them to complete reading the books they have chosen and write a report at the end, don't you?

A: I would like for them to finish reading the book if they choose to, but I do not want to request a written report. I just want us to focus on their experiences as readers.

Several teachers offered to assist, and when a parent volunteered to donate juice and muffins each week, we were on our way. I decided to call it the Breakfast Bunche Literacy Club (BBLC) to honor Ralph Bunche—educator, civil rights leader, and the 1950 Nobel Peace Prize laureate.

The idea of a book club had come to me unexpectedly while I was wrestling with ways to expand students' language and thinking. My introspective nature makes me curious about the motivations of others—how they think and why they think that way. I wanted to know about the students' meaning-making strategies and how they used them to develop oral and print competencies in literacy. Exploring these ideas in the social context of a book club was a way of offering children a different kind of learning environment for developing literacy and language skills. In addition, it also offered an opportunity for me to expand my role as a speech-language pathologist and assume a broader and more integral role in the school's literacy program.

There were two requirements for membership in the book club: (1) The child likes to read, and (2) the child likes to talk. All readers were welcome regardless of reading and oral language ability. My thinking was that talk among students about their reading would enhance their reading experiences and fuel their passion to read more. Students might inspire others to read books that they might not otherwise have chosen. In our Readers as Teachers and Teachers as Readers seminar, we did those things: We talked about books and magazine and newspaper articles, and often someone in the group would decide to read what someone else was enthusiastic about. This is natural among avid readers. Adult readers do not have to write a book report to show that they have taken something away from their reading. Yes, writing serves to help clarify one's thinking; however, the formality of a book report is not always necessary as a means for sharing meaningful experiences with books.

Students might inspire others to read books that they might not otherwise have chosen.

The children in the BBLC responded enthusiastically. Their discussions about self-chosen books were lively and responsive. I attempted to recreate the inviting setting modeled in my graduate seminar by having music play softly as my students arrived. As we enjoyed our music, muffins, and juice, we talked. "Books make us dream and imagine that we are different people in different places," said one student. They even asked if they could read my book, *Take a Lesson: Today's Black Achievers on How They Made It and What They Learned Along the Way* by Caroline V. Clarke (2000). This surprised me because I expected that they would only choose to read books their peers liked. They did not seem intimidated by the thickness of my book or the difficulties they might have reading it. Inspired by them, I read aloud a selection that I found to be inspiring and to communicate, "Yes, this is a book that you can choose to read one day!"

The third-grade students continued to surprise me. We agreed to "be slow to say that a book was no good," and several students said they were not discouraged when someone expressed displeasure with a particular book selection. Actually, they felt challenged to read the book and form their own opinions, adding more good talk about unique relationships between people and books. One student expressed personal value placed in reading by exclaiming, "I read in the morning, before I go to bed at night, and when I'm on the bus. I read because there are words!"

Students talked about what books made them think about. After reading *Little House in the Big Woods* (Wilder, 1971), one student said, "It makes you feel how hard it is to be poor. We should probably help them." Another responded, "If someone were poor, I'd let them live with me and try to build them a house." These comments led me to tell about the organization called Habitat for Humanity, which brings community members together to build houses for people who are poor or homeless.

Our principal, instructional lead teacher, and a retired classroom teacher all had come to share their reading with us. After the retired teacher shared her enthusiasm about a book, one child told us, "I was the first one to check it out. I was so excited. I stayed up all night reading." Then, another student shared how her dad stayed up all night reading a book. One boy said, "That book I was reading last time, called *Redwall* [Jacques, 1986], I couldn't take my eyes off it. I had to force myself to put it down." Of course, I shared my all-night experience with *Before Women Had Wings*. Ten students raised their hands to say that they had stayed up all night reading books. Our conversations were recursive and wove together readers' experiences, books, authors, community, homes, and families.

Students questioned one another in ways that paralleled questions I traditionally asked my students:

"Why did you choose that book?"

"Did you enjoy reading that book?"

"What made you read that book?"

"What was your favorite part?"

"Can we read a page from our book?"

Time and space seemed suspended when we came together as a community of readers. I felt that it was important to take my reading back to the students and share ways that reading influenced my life. In doing so, I found out more about students and how they learned from their reading experiences. When I share with students how I am affected by an author who uses language to create imagery in poignant ways or how I use critical reflections of text to consider my life, I communicate that the educational goals we hold are important throughout life. I have a revised professional goal based on my experience with the Readers as Teachers and Teachers as Readers seminar and my BBLC: I want to be prepared to guide students toward alternative perspectives and lead them toward broader ways of thinking. To do this, I must continually strive to read to lead. Over 40 students from 4 third-grade classes joined the BBLC. The students have shared that they wish we could meet more often than once a month, and so do I. We shall see.

> Time and space seemed suspended when we came together as a community of readers.

LITERATURE CITED

Clarke, C.V. (2000). *Take a lesson: Today's black achievers on how they made it and what they learned along the way.* New York: Wiley.

Fowler, C.M. (1996). *Before women had wings.* New York: Putnam.

Fowler, C.M. (2000). *Remembering Blue.* New York: Doubleday.

Jacques, B. (1986). *Redwall.* New York: Philomel.

Park, B. (1987). *The kid in the red jacket.* New York: Random House.

Wilder, L.I. (1971). *Little house in the big woods.* New York: HarperCollins.

—Betty Hubbard—
UNIVERSITY TEACHER

Betty has been teaching at the college level for four years. She has taught multiple courses on content area literacy to undergraduate students at the University of Georgia. She also has taught developmental reading at the college level.

Initially, Betty enrolled in the Readers as Teachers and Teachers as Readers seminar because she was eager to keep in touch with other teachers and was very curious about the course. Her favorite reading from the seminar was the article, "Pondering the ubiquity of reading: What can we learn?" (2001), written by the leader of the seminar, Michelle Commeyras. Betty enjoyed this article because she fully realized the role reading can play in the construction of self and how she might use that information in her own classroom.

—Dawn Spruill—
ASSISTANT PRINCIPAL

Dawn began her career by working for six years in accounting and banking. Before becoming a teacher, she spent a year as paraprofessional and two years as the attendance registrar in the Barrow County, Georgia, school system. Then, she began seven years as a classroom teacher in first, second, fourth, and fifth grades. She is now an assistant principal at Walker Park Elementary School in Monroe, Georgia.

Taking the seminar allowed Dawn to rediscover her love of reading and made her realize that reading was what drew her to education in the first place.

Dawn's favorite readings from the Readers as Teachers and Teachers as Readers seminar were BEFORE WOMEN HAD WINGS by Connie May Fowler (1996) and ELLEN FOSTER by Kaye Gibbons (1987). She still has a long list of recommended reading from the seminar discussions.

CHAPTER 10

Stories That Fund Experience

Betty Hubbard and Dawn Spruill

We (Dawn and Betty H.) arrived at the same place at the same time, exploring reading in our professional and personal lives and examining what it means to be teachers who identify themselves as readers and who teach reading. We found ourselves talking often about relationships in our lives, and we discovered reading was a central factor in many of our relationships. For us, reading is often the catalyst for union, the cement that unites and binds relationships. There are no rules for the formation of these relationships; they simply emerge from sharing stories.

Stories enrapture us, propel us forward, lead us to seek more in a quest to satiate the unquenchable. We are compelled to build this reverence for stories in students. Is this informed passion or random lunacy? This is not something we had thought about before in the company of professional others. We knew from experience that reading is a necessary component for academic success, but this shared impetus comes from the depths; it is urgent, essential, and basic.

We believe that sharing stories opens us to change, melding the disparity of culture and preference. The written word bears transformative power forceful enough to ground visions of social change, yet gentle enough to plant the seeds of understanding. Stories position us in time, space, gender, race, ideology, and pedagogy. We have laughed, cried, and befriended characters and authors we will never meet. Still, we reserve a place for them at our conversation tables. Carrying their wisdom with us, we whittle away at the splintered edges of our person, reshaping our subjectivities and smoothing our rough ideas into newly fashioned, more informed dispositions. Our readings challenge us to question the

> The written word bears transformative power forceful enough to ground visions of social change, yet gentle enough to plant the seeds of understanding.

origins of our ideas and interrogate our assumptions. This is our quest. We share our explorations here.

Contemplating beginnings, Dawn wrote the following narrative to share with Betty H. after attending a class at Metro Regional Educational Service Agency in northwest Atlanta, housed in a former school that bears a striking resemblance to her first elementary school:

I was filled with a sense of nostalgia and déjà vu. Classrooms in these buildings have high ceilings, transoms to the hallway, several large chalkboards with narrow corkboards on top, and two or three shallow closets along one wall. These closets held supplies, books, and the glue we all loved to eat in primary school. The windows to the outside are tall and still hold attachments for the canvas blinds that raise and lower from the center point of the window. The little girl that I was whispers in my ear as we share our memories of those days. In the transom, I see my best friend's dusty, yellow flip-flop sandal, thrown there by the boy who loved to tease. I remember my anger with that boy and the teacher because they didn't seem to care that my friend was crying.

I recall the clicking, ticking radiators; the creaking of the wooden floors; the smell of chalk dust and mold; and the bathrooms with the plywood stalls and short sinks. The tall, low-to-the-ground windows remind me of being the classroom fire marshal. My job was to check the hallway door with my hand. If it was hot, we had to climb out the windows to safety during a fire drill. My little friend and I giggled about how our teacher must have hated the month when it was my turn as class fire marshal!

I remember recess under the tall oaks, enjoying tea with acorns and leaves for our china. Our school had a treasure trove of books in the library, but no librarian. When we finished our work early, we were able to explore the prairie with Laura Ingalls Wilder or blaze a new trail with Daniel Boone.

Now, dimmed by my administrative responsibilities as an assistant principal, I realize what is not remembered. I cannot remember details of day-to-day classroom instructions. How did I learn about letters and the magical way they come together to form reading experiences? Although I don't remember a single reading lesson in that elementary school, I do remember coming home to read about Dick and Jane with my parents. I wanted to be a teacher. I loved school and the sights, sounds, and smells of school—whether they are memories of past schools or the day-to-day occurrences in my current school. I never really went away from that school, and doubt that I ever will.

Beginnings for Betty H. were quite different. She hated school—the sounds, sights, smells, rules, and rigidity—as demonstrated in the following narrative she shared with Dawn:

All too often I found myself in the coat closet for disrupting the class. It was all so confusing. One minute, I was reprimanded for talking and amid my resolve to remain quiet, I realized the teacher was again yelling at me for talking. It was impossible to pay attention. I heard the clock tick away endless minutes; the boy on my left scratching his thigh; the girl behind me turning pages in her workbook; and on my right, someone tapping a pencil. Others were clicking tongues, coughing, breathing audibly.

Hypersensitive and overstimulated, I heard and saw everything at once. I felt imprisoned by a desk that was too big, too hard, and too cold. Further enslaved by test scores that revealed "ability," I learned that I was inattentive and unproductive. School was boring, I couldn't think; the pace was tortuously slow. I had been reminded too many times to stay with the class. How could I? They did the same thing for hours. I wanted to. I wanted to "be good," to do as the others did "to live up to my potential," as I so often heard. But what does that mean? It was as if everyone but me had a copy of the rules. I learned them eventually, but only after I had broken them.

It was among the coats, hats, and mittens that I learned to read. The coat closet was a quiet room, a free-standing wall with one window and no doors. Winter wear hanging on hooks provided acoustics from the dullness of the lessons. Extra books were stored on shelves, and if I was very quiet, I could remove them one by one, crawl between the pages, and emerge among the legends and biographies. I began reading pictures, then matching words to pictures. Once I realized that I truly was reading, I bolted to the door to share the news. However, because I had not paid attention in class, I was not attended to. So reading became my secret—my personal coup to disrupt the tedium. Perhaps I was not learning the valued curriculum; I was, however, making meaning of the lessons available to me. I sensed, more than knew, the magnitude of my discovery.

Enchanted, enthralled, and excited, I turned each page, watching the letters align themselves into words and those words into sentences. In awe, I remembered my kindergarten teacher and her gentle admonishment the previous year when I carelessly tossed a book onto the floor, "We are always careful with our books. They are our friends." Now I understood; now I had a reason to be here. I began to develop a purpose for learning. I began to develop me.

I wonder now if my reading teacher knew what she was doing. Perhaps she stacked those books in the closet, intentionally orchestrating my rebellion. To date, when I pass a child sitting in the hall, ostracized for disruptive behavior, I wonder what would happen if her teacher removed her with a book in hand? I wonder because I hold reading in great esteem and believe it to be central to who I am, who I can become, and what I have to offer others. Reading functions, I believe, as a metaphor for life: as life is, as life can be, and, in particular, as life can never be. In other words, I am shaped by the lessons I take from the stories I encounter.

> "I began to develop a purpose for learning. I began to develop me."

This experience is the opportunity we wanted to offer our students. We pondered the question, How can we create an environment that uncovers the magic and potential of reading for our students? Considering this, Dawn reflected on how reading affected her actions as an assistant principal by recalling a particularly busy day.

One night as Dawn left class, she noticed the full moon floating in the sky. It glowed huge and mysterious—a true harvest moon. Some nights she doesn't know the moon is full because she's not outside to see it. Other nights, she drags herself home, knowing the moon is full, not because she saw it, but because she dealt with full moon craziness all day. That was one of those days! She drove to work with nothing on her mind except the five student support team (SST) meetings she must chair, a proposal she had to present for funds to support a landscaping project, the collaborative reading class she would teach in fourth grade, and the work she needed to complete for her university classes. Dawn expected this to be a normal day. Was she listening to the radio? Was she listening to an audiobook? Dawn doesn't remember, but she does know that she didn't notice that sly man in the moon leering over her shoulder and was woefully unprepared for what was to follow.

On arrival, a teacher notified Dawn that a student had brought a knife to school and made a threatening comment to a classmate. This may be a normal occurrence in some schools, but not at Dawn's school. Zero-tolerance laws say any potential weapon is *not* innocent. The day was beginning to seem like a roller coaster ride. First, there was an unscheduled hour of paperwork, then a report that a student had tried to pass a bad check at the book fair. What was going on? Dawn's is a small rural community school, and such incidents are unusual. Another round of calls, investigations, and tears ensued. Dawn still hadn't looked at the calendar, but she had a sneaking suspicion that they were experiencing abnormal lunar interference.

Two teacher observations, then Dawn was off to the fourth-grade classroom where she was teaching a collaborative reading unit. The students were excited about the book they were reading and that was Dawn's goal—getting students excited about reading and the difference it can make in their lives. She also wanted to share the experience with her teachers because she believes that reading from quality children's literature is an extremely important dimension in any method of teaching reading.

That evening, in our graduate seminar, the class discussed a video about Rae Ellen McKee, a national teacher of the year. McKee asks all her students, "How do you want to be when you grow up?" The most touching answer came from McKee's own daughter who replies, "I want to be full of me."

Dawn is grown up but continues to reflect about how she wants to be. Is the life she lives now what she would have chosen if she were a child again? Is she "full of me"? On days like those full-moon days, when Dawn reaches home feeling like she's been on a wild ride, she wonders if this is how she wants to be.

One benefit of our Readers as Teachers seminar has been the almost unending list of books that Dawn wants to read. Two of these, *Ellen Foster* (Gibbons, 1987) and *Before Women Had Wings* (Fowler, 1996) spoke to Dawn as a reader, a teacher, and an administrator. In both books, the teacher and other adults influence the young female characters. Dawn wondered if her interventions and teaching had similarly influenced the student who carried the knife to school or the one who tried to pass a bad check. What impression had she made on the students in the fourth-grade reading class? What was she unaware of? Was her influence positive or negative? After such a day, Dawn realized anew how reading shapes her perceptions. She had never experienced poverty or neglect, or struggled in school; she did experience such things through reading about other lives. Dawn came to a deeper understanding of the lives of her students and teachers. Her reading helps her be more effective and empathetic as she deals with students for whom such struggles are an everyday occurrence. Dawn encourages her teachers to use reading as a means to expand children's experiences. In this way, each child may get a glimpse of alternate lives and possibilities. Reading opens doors that can become opportunities for growth, understanding, and tolerance. This is the beauty of reading, in our estimation.

Meanwhile Betty H. wondered about the college students she teaches: "Who are these people?" she asked herself. It mattered who they were. And it mattered that Betty H. saw through the selves they sometimes presented into the selves they wanted to become. Perhaps it was her opportunity to provide context and texts that helped them forge those identities. Betty H. learned from reading *A Hope in the Unseen* (1998), Ron Suskind's Pulitzer Prize-winning ethnographic novel, that students have good reasons for what they say and do—reasons we cannot always understand. Suskind recounts the experience of Cedric, an inner-city African American youth, and his struggle to transcend

> *Reading opens doors that can become opportunities for growth, understanding, and tolerance.*

circumstance and earn an Ivy League education. Although it is important to establish trust in the classroom, it is also important to trust our students. Cedric has no reason to believe that his efforts will be rewarded, yet he learns how to negotiate the twists and turns that threaten to snare him—the other crabs in the bucket, as he calls them, those that would repeatedly pull him back as he reaches beyond the rim toward a future self. Who are the Cedrics in Betty H.'s class? Who are the students masked for reasons of their own—reasons that may help them climb out of their buckets? Through the readings Betty H. assigned, many of them saw the rims on their own, reading about similar but different entrapments.

Students in Betty H.'s content literacy class were learning about the discursive practices of historical interpretation. Betty asked them to read multiple conflicting sources about a historic event and consider how past historic events informed current decisions regarding U.S. foreign and domestic policy. Each class, students shared something they had read relating to this objective. As they discussed alternatives and interpretations, Betty H. noticed that students were bringing in articles to share and asking one another about sources so they could read more about the people of Afghanistan and issues that led to current international crises. They were interested, and they were reading!

Moreover, students were writing about their interpretations in their learning journals, which contained weekly reflections recounting their thoughts, feelings, and insights as a result of their learning experiences. Katherine (pseudonym), a preservice teacher in her senior year, wrote that she felt ashamed because she had no idea that people were enduring such hardships:

> How could I have been so oblivious to these atrocities? I realize that I have a responsibility to read more, question more, and think about the effect my words and decisions have on those around me. I may not be able to make a difference now, but I hope to teach one day. Then I will caution my students to think about both sides of the issues they are confronted with. It simply never occurred to me before now that we had any responsibility that contributed to the terrible conditions in Afghanistan. I have been terribly naïve. I am terribly ashamed of being so self-centered.

Justin, a sophomore majoring in business, wrote the following:

> I have actually enjoyed reading about the current crisis we are
> faced with and looking for the reasons political advisors are
> thinking and reacting in certain ways. I wonder what I would
> do in similar circumstances? As a student my options are
> limited. I can avoid buying Nikes because children are forced
> to work in sweatshops that manufacture them, but my
> options are somewhat limited otherwise. As far as how it will
> affect me professionally in the workforce, if I ever deal with
> those companies that do business with or support an
> oppressive regime, I may choose *not* to deal with them
> because I know that they are harming innocent civilians in
> their countries. The issues I am reading about are helping me
> decide how I want to act as a professional. I guess I am really
> thinking about things more deeply.

Stories such as the ones Betty H.'s students read and wrote
about fund experience. Experience, Betty believes, *is* education.
Not all experience qualifies; certain criteria must be met to provide
authentic experience or quality experience. Experience occasions
growth and opens growth in new directions. Thus, experience has
the quality of continuity in a temporary sense. As an educator, Betty
knows it is up to her to manipulate the classroom environment to
fund experience in ways that allow for continuity and interaction.
Funded experience can be the vicarious learning that takes place
between the student and a knowledgeable other. The student
integrates the experience of this other into his or her knowledge
base and uses it in future endeavors to react or think in new ways.

Betty H. wrote about these ideas in the following narrative
that she shared with Dawn after a recent trip to Mexico:

> On the Yucatan peninsula, where warm turquoise water rolls
> over bleached-white rocky shorelines, I sat perched on a half-
> submerged timeworn stone, watching the seaweed unwind and
> wind again around my ankles in rhythm with the waves. I
> wondered how it must have been 2000 years ago. Did Mayan
> mothers sit in this same spot watching their children play in the
> surf? Or, were they relegated to those cliffs high above the
> rocky beaches watching from the now-crumbling pyramids? I
> can easily imagine the pinnacle that once stood atop those
> pyramids, pinnacles that time transformed into now-rounded

trapezoidal shapes. And although time barters with the appearance of this abandoned land, in exchange, it embeds significance and meaning in the stories left behind. It is a sort of currency, diffuse yet palpable, veiling each visitor in reverence as he or she enters the stone archway into the courtyard of ruins. Mothers hush children, and adults communicate wordlessly, as though they were entering the sanctuary of an ancient cathedral. Even the tour guides, repeating their mantras, shepherd listeners with gestures and hushed tones. There is a sense of respect for those who came before us, those who transcend time through stone-carved words, sharing themselves in their stories. I wondered what prompted them to record aspects of their culture. Reading the myths and legends of this ancient culture, I realized many cultures share common themes. Across the time and space of centuries, stories of origin and creation vary by detail but not by the need to explain universe and existence. It is through the telling and reading of these stories that one age can know the pain and passions of another. Mayan stories, like ours, relay tradition, instill morals, and bind future generations to ancestors, offering heritage and meaning through a sense of connectedness. I feel closer to them and have a greater sense of who I want to be.

This is the beauty of reading, in our estimation. Stories have the flexibility to meet students where they are developmentally, emotionally, and cognitively. Students take whatever lessons they've learned from others' experiences that connect with their own previous experiences and can be used as ways to understand and validate their current experiences. In this way, successive experiences are integrated into one another. Thus, reading becomes the study of experience, and it dispels apathy through a sense of historical connectedness.

REFERENCES

Commeyras, M. (2001). Pondering the ubiquity of reading: What can we learn? *Journal of Adolescent & Adult Literacy, 44,* 520–524.

LITERATURE CITED

Fowler, C.M. (1996). *Before women had wings.* New York: Putnam.
Gibbons, K. (1987). *Ellen Foster.* Chapel Hill, NC: Algonquin Books.
Suskind, R. (1998). *A hope in the unseen: An American odyssey from the inner city to the Ivy League.* New York: Broadway Books.

—Jill Hermann-Wilmarth—
TEACHER EDUCATOR

Jill has taught fourth and fifth grades and a multiage second- and third-grade classroom. She is currently working with preservice teachers at the University of Georgia. She teaches children's literature and language arts methods classes.

Her favorite reading from the Readers as Teachers and Teachers as Readers seminar was WOUNDS OF PASSION: THE WRITING LIFE by bell hooks (1997). Jill loves memoirs, and this one really shed light on how when writing, reading, and living are integrated, living can be richer, thinking can be clearer, and connections to people and events can be made stronger.

CHAPTER 11

Risky Teaching

Jill Hermann-Wilmarth

I t is harried. Students from my class wait for the previous group to clear their books and conversations from the room so in the next five minutes, we can rearrange the tables into *our* configuration. My 27 students proceed to cluster in their usual groups. As teacher of this undergraduate children's literature class, I attempt to organize the piles that I lug to class every day—our read-aloud book, picture books that reflect the genre of focus for the day, texts that I'm reading that have inspired me and that I want to share, graded papers, and roll sheets. After checking my watch, I close the door at exactly 10:10 a.m., while the story exchange that occurs continues among this cohort of students who know one another well. Their broad cultural similarities (all white, except one woman who moved to the United States from Korea as a young child; mostly Christian except for two students who are practicing Jews; and mostly middle class—their trendy clothing, expensive backpacks, and jingling car keys reveal more than a sense of fashion) camouflage the more subtle experiential differences that could bring a sense of diversity to our class discussions. I feel a sense of nervousness about the challenge that I am about to initiate—asking class participants, myself included, to step out of comfort zones and think about privilege in a way that explores the role of that privilege in our lives as teachers of diverse student populations. I hope to support this risk taking through dialogue about children's literature that is considered controversial. I hope that by beginning with small groups of friends, the students will first be able to take risks in our relatively safe classroom setting and later take risks in the classroom communities that they establish with their own students.

But, where is *my* relatively safe classroom setting? How can I explore what it will mean to take risks with my students, without feeling so exposed? When I sat in our Readers as Teachers and Teachers as Readers seminar on the first night, I realized that I was surrounded by teachers who were trying new things with their students, too. Each reader in the seminar somehow wanted to change her teaching so her students would feel the excitement of reading and would become better readers with lives as enriched as ours—with stories and notions and facts that we find in our reading lives and then integrate into our daily living. *This* was my relatively safe classroom setting. Here was where I could test some possible responses to my shared reading life, to my risky literature. Here it felt invigorating to look at my teaching through the lens of my reading. In this class of very different teachers who share a very similar passion for really good books, trying something new was the norm. That insecure, "Should I be stepping out on this limb?" look wasn't only on my face but on the face of all the readers as teachers in our class. Sharing the responses of our students helped me see that I wasn't going at it alone.

The undergraduate class I teach has a Monday morning ritual. Right after our read-aloud and response, we separate into groups of five, trying to not sit with colleagues with whom we have shared before. We each bring to the group one of our own cultural artifacts, and with that artifact, thoughts about why it represents a part of us in a meaningful way and how the culture that it represents is portrayed in public school and in children's literature. These 10 minutes of time are intended to build bridges among our commonalities and differences. My cultural artifact one Monday morning was the wedding invitation that my spouse, Jessica, and I created. To me, it represents not only my pride in who I am as a lesbian but also my sense of spirituality, my socioeconomic privilege, and my strong family connections.

> In this class of very different teachers who share a very similar passion for really good books, trying something new was the norm.

I was full of nervous tension, of not knowing—a little bit like what Liza must feel when she first reads the phone message left by her mother in *Annie on My Mind* (Garden, 1982):

> I don't know why, but as soon as I saw that note, I felt my
> heart starting to beat faster. I also realized I was now
> thoroughly glad Mom wasn't home, because I didn't want
> anyone around when I called Annie, though again I didn't
> know why. My mouth felt dry, so I got a drink of water, and I
> almost dropped the glass because my hands were suddenly
> sweaty. (p. 32)

This book is the story of the risk of Liza's exploration of sexual
identity, but what would my sharing—my risking—do to our
classroom dynamics? It felt risky to me to share this part of who I
am with my students. Would I be seen differently? Would I be less
trusted? Would my students care?

Risk: What is it? At one moment, it is challenging cultural
norms by expressing the expectation that students not only tolerate
but respect and learn with someone who is openly different than
they are and whose very way of being in the world might disrupt
some of their belief systems. In another equally valid and tense
moment, risk is challenging a school's cultural norms by integrating
literature into a social studies curriculum. Does *my* definition of risk
mean pushing the boundaries of a particular context beyond what is
considered the norm? How will these two moments—my students'
and mine, defined only by a shared feeling—affect our teaching
and learning?

I was a successful student in classrooms where status quo
teaching was the norm. I also grew up in a place of incredible racial
and economic privilege. If my teachers did not take risks in their
teaching and did not ask me to think outside the dominant cultural
paradigm, I was not one of the students who would slip through the
cracks. I was a student who, for the most part, had no worries or
fears of being forgotten. My married, heterosexual, white, upper-
middle-class parents made sure that I did my homework, that I was
read to, and that I had access to a variety of cultural activities. Even
if my feminist voice was not completely valued at home or at
school, as I got older I had access to spaces where it would not be
completely silenced. But what will happen to students who don't

have that privilege and whose experiences of society are much more marginalized than those of a white, wealthy, feminist lesbian?

I want to learn with my students, to teach in ways that do not discount the cultures of those who sit outside the dominant paradigm. In her essay "La Guerra," Cherríe Moraga (1983) writes,

> I have come to believe that the only reason women of a privileged class will dare to look at how it is that they oppress, is when they've come to know the meaning of their own oppression. And understand that the oppression of others hurts them personally. (p. 33)

I agree. I believe that until preservice teachers, or teachers and students in general, who are steeped in privilege, are forced to read or hear or think about the oppression that historically stems from the systems that have given them that privilege, they will, subconsciously or not, perpetuate these systems. Likewise, I fear that students who do not have racial or economic privilege, but who are forced to sit in classrooms where their status as oppressed or marginalized people is perpetuated will internalize the racism or sexism or homophobia or classism that they face daily in schools. Audre Lorde (1979) writes that

> as women, we have been taught to either ignore our differences or to view them as causes for separation and suspicion rather than as forces for change. Without community, there is no liberation, only the most vulnerable and temporary armistice between an individual and her oppression. But community must not mean a shedding of our differences, nor the pathetic pretense that these differences do not exist. (p. 99)

It is the responsibility of the teacher to help create communities in which students can both retain their diverse identities and feel valued because of them. A first step toward becoming a teacher who can and will create this kind of community is to read and think outside of one's culture. This potential discomfort—this opportunity to challenge the normalization of one's own culture—is key to growth. And if disharmony, in a relatively safe space (my classroom, where we've built a trusting community), helps my students become better teachers to those traditionally marginalized, then that discomfort plays an important role.

During their second semester of education classes, my students spend a month in the field, observing and participating in classrooms in local elementary schools. This is the first time they have a formal teaching observation by one of their professors. My ritual, as an observer, is to spend a scheduled hour in the classroom, taking copious notes as the student teaches a well-planned and reviewed lesson. We then sit together and debrief the experience, sharing our thoughts, feelings, and ideas about how the lesson played out. During one such debriefing session after the observation of a social studies lesson, I suggested to one student that she could use some children's literature in her teaching of maps and landforms. "After all," I said, "I am a resource for you and would love to help you do that." My student—who is moved by powerful literature, who borrows books that I share from my reading life, who writes inspired poetry about characters that she met in *Bridge to Terabithia* (Paterson, 1976) and *The Watsons Go to Birmingham—1963: A Novel* (Curtis, 1997)—looked me straight in the eye during that debriefing and told me that she had thought of integrating literature, particularly with me coming to observe, but within the context of that classroom, it felt too risky. She wanted to stick with what was the norm in another teacher's classroom.

Every literacy event in which I participate has the power to alter my life perspective and to alter my perspectives of what it means to be a teacher or a student. As a teacher and a researcher, I am interested in how risk taking by members of learning communities in colleges and elementary schools expands student understandings. I find myself constantly drawn to the children's and young adult sections of bookstores, looking for books that have been challenged or whose characters live lives that my students and I may never understand or experience because of the cultures in which we live. Anyone thumbing through the books on my shelves would be exposed to the commonalities that I feel toward the feelings or thoughts of the characters by the stars, words of agreement or question, and double underlines that I've marked in the text and on the margins of the pages. I do this reading both for my own enjoyment and to find texts that might challenge and inspire my thinking, and thus my student's thinking, about children's literature.

I want to learn with my students, to teach in ways that do not discount the cultures of those who sit outside the dominant paradigm.

I have been reading feminist theory, and it feeds my pedagogy in interesting ways. Texts such as *A Room of One's Own* (Woolf, 1929/1967), *Ain't I a Woman: Black Women and Feminism* (hooks, 1981), and *This Bridge Called My Back: Writings by Radical Women of Color* (Moraga & Anzaldua, 1983), and selections from *New French Feminisms* (Marks & de Courtivron, 1980) are full of narrative histories, poetry, manifestos, and journals about women who take risks by writing and living their truths in ways that subvert dominant expectations of them as women, or women of color, or lesbians, or poor women. These writings also describe how that risk changed lives. To me, the call of these and other female authors encourages me to take risks in my life, in my classroom, in my learning, and in my writing and to encourage my students to do the same as they continue on their paths toward elementary school teaching. Virginia Woolf writes in 1929 of the missing stories of women and that "looking about the shelves for books that were not there," it "would be ambitious beyond [her] daring" (1929/1967, p. 45) to try to fill this void. *Ain't I a Woman: Black Women and Feminism* seems to take this ambition to heart, as bell hooks shares the lives of women whose existence has been long ignored because of their race, class, and gender. Likewise, Helene Cixous (1976) calls women "to sing, to write, to dare to speak, in short, to bring out something new" (p. 246) because, she says, "A feminine text cannot fail to be more than subversive. It is volcanic; as it is written it brings about an upheaval" (p. 258). These words and actions inspire me to take risks, to cause upheaval in my teaching and in my interactions with my students, but it is not easy. I hope to call my students to teach in the ways that these feminists have encouraged women to write and speak, to listen and live. In order to do this, I want to think about the context of our class and how reading and sharing our reading lives as teachers of children's literature provide spaces for that risk. As their teacher, I hold and I believe in the ultimate responsibility to model "risky" behavior. What will this mean for me as a teacher, as a student? What will it mean for my students?

It is through my lens of privilege and marginalization that I see and live everything, including teaching. As a student, I have felt attacked when I spoke openly from my experience as a lesbian by those with conservative religious beliefs. I have sat silently out of fear as a teacher and as a student. These experiences affect my view of students who speak freely about their fundamentalist religious views. I bristle because I do not feel that I am allowed the same privilege. I have had a few students who were willing to step back from the privilege of being part of the dominant culture to look at how marginalized students might experience the same classrooms that they excelled in. I now expect that most university students studying to be elementary teachers will resist my pushing them to question their privileges as middle-class, white, Christian, heterosexual women.

When my students returned to my class from a month of practice teaching, I shared a book with them that some might consider controversial. When Mildred Taylor's *The Friendship* (1987) was read by elementary and middle school teachers in a graduate course I took, there were mixed responses about the appropriateness of using the book with schoolchildren. Taylor tells the powerful story of a so-called friendship between a black Tom Bee—and a white man—John Wallace—in 1933 Mississippi. The title gives me, as a reader, a false sense of hope, and my need for a happy ending is denied by the racism of Wallace.

I wanted my students, in reading this book, to gain a historical view as college students in a southern university with a racist past and also a greater understanding of the lives of their future African American students and colleagues. The book *is* uncomfortable in its honesty. I am hoping that this discomfort lends itself to what Laurel Richardson describes as "writing as a way of knowing" (2000, p. 923). Knowing and learning how and why they have privilege and power through the hearing and writing of risky words might encourage my students to become risky teachers. I hope that it encourages the action of teachers who don't necessarily follow status quo teaching practices, but who create with their students curricula that allow for critical questioning and action in classrooms.

In the foreword to the second edition of *This Bridge Called My Back*, Moraga (1983) writes,

Knowing and learning how and why they have privilege and power through the hearing and writing of risky words might encourage my students to become risky teachers.

> The political writer...is the ultimate optimist, believing people are capable of change and using words as one way to try and penetrate the privatism of our lives. A privatism that keeps us back and away from each other, which renders us politically useless. (n.p.)

The political teacher, then, the risky teacher, uses the words of powerful and challenging literature to push himself or herself and his or her students into ways of thinking that confront the status quo. Risky teachers, risky readers. Readers who teach and teachers who read risk making a difference.

REFERENCES

Cixous, H. (1980). The laugh of the medusa. In E. Marks, I. de Courtivron (Eds.), *New French feminisms* (pp. 245–264). New York: Shocken Books.

hooks, b. (1981). *Ain't I a woman? Black women and feminism*. Boston: South End Press.

hooks, b. (1997). *Wounds of passion: A writing life*. New York: Henry Holt.

Lorde, A. (1983). The master's tools will never dismantle the master's house: Comments at "The personal and the political" panel. In C. Moraga, & G. Anzaldua (Eds.), *This bridge called my back: Writings by radical women of color* (pp. 98–101). New York: Kitchen Table: Women of Color Press.

Marks, E., & de Courtivron, I. (Eds.). (1980). *New French feminisms*. New York: Shocken Books.

Moraga, C. (1983). La Guerra. In C. Moraga, & G. Anzaldua (Eds.), *This bridge called my back: Writings by radical women of color* (pp. 27–34). New York: Kitchen Table: Women of Color Press.

Moraga, C. (1983). Refugees of a world on fire: Foreword to the second edition. In C. Moraga, & G. Anzaldua (Eds.), *This bridge called my back: Writings by radical women of color*. New York: Kitchen Table: Women of Color Press.

Richardson, L. (2000). Writing: A method of inquiry. In N.K. Denzin & Y.S. Lincoln (Eds.), *Handbook of qualitative research*. (2nd ed., pp. 923–948). Thousand Oaks, CA: Sage.

Woolf, V. (1967). *A room of one's own*. London: Hogarth Press. (Original work published 1929)

LITERATURE CITED

Curtis, C.P. (1997). *The Watsons go to Birmingham—1963: A novel*. New York: Bantam.

Garden, N. (1982). *Annie on my mind*. New York: Aerial Fiction.

Paterson, K. (1976). *Bridge to Terabithia*. New York: Harper.

Taylor, M. (1987). *The friendship*. New York: Dial.

—Margret Echols—
PREKINDERGARTEN TEACHER

Most of Margret's teaching experience for the last nine years has been with prekindergarten students. At present, she is also working with kindergartners in the 21st Century Community Learning Centers of McDuffie County, Georgia.

Margret recalls that class time in the seminar never seemed to be long enough:

> Often before class would begin, we would write on the board quotes from our readings that we wanted to share with the class. This proved to be wonderful "sampling" time. I can remember scrambling to write down all the words and phrases that spoke to me and realizing that I needed to find a central place to keep these words and phrases alongside ones I'd discovered in my own reading journeys, so that I could visit them again and again. It was like a box of assorted chocolates being placed in the hands of a "chocoholic," enticing me to sample so many other books that were being devoured by other readers.

Margret's favorite reading from the Readers as Teachers and Teachers as Readers seminar was ELLEN FOSTER by Kaye Gibbons (1987) because it touched all her emotions. Margret was captivated by the main character, Ellen, who stole her heart.

CHAPTER 12

My Reading Pleasures: My Self, My Child, My Family, My Students

Margret Echols

What is that thing?
You hold tight in your hand
That takes you
To some other land
What is that thing?
Reflecting in your eyes,
Spilling from your lips
Weaving through your mind.
Swiftly your eyes cross each line,
Your fingers lift page after page
A rhythm in time
Pages, pictures, words
They speak loudly
With hardly a sound
Eyes focused
Fingers twitching
Heart pounding
Laughs, sighs, and tears
When it's not open
It's close to your heart.

Please share it
I simply must know
About that thing you hold in your hand.

Have you ever watched someone who is engaged in reading a book? It is so amazing to see a reader so totally engrossed in what he or she is reading. I tried to capture this image in the poem above. Sometimes you see it in the reader's eyes as he peers above the top of the book, in the tension in his forehead, or in the fluid movements of his lips as they pore over every word. You can tell that the reader is held captive to the words on the pages, completely unaware of the surrounding world.

It is these very reading pleasures that I long for when I see others reading and when I am reading a book of my own. These are also the very pleasures I want my husband, my children, and my students to know and thirst for.

I love to read. I love children's books. I love books that make me cry and make me laugh. I love books that make me question. As a teacher in an elementary school, I see struggling readers all the time. For them, reading is a chore. I see children that can't read but want to. I see children that can read but don't. This tragedy inspires me as a prekindergarten teacher to lead every one of my very young students to experience the joy a book can bring. I am constantly trying to figure out how I can spark their interest in books and, more important, in reading, especially as they become ready for more formal reading instruction.

My own reading unexpectedly inspires me. The following excerpt from *Ellen Foster* by Kaye Gibbons (1987) is a good example:

> I could lay here all night. I am not able to fall asleep without reading. You have that time when your brain has nothing constructive to do so it rambles. I fool my brain out of that by making it read until it shuts off. I just think it is best to do something right up until you fall asleep. (p. 10)

I realize that looking at myself as a reader leads me to realize ways of being a model for my students. I want to find out what my children think about this thing called reading and if they see me as a reader. Making myself more visible as a reader could be a way for me to better communicate my love of reading with them. I remember my mother and my grandmother having books in our home, visiting the library, and reading to me. I also had a special friend who could read faster than I did, so I got her to read to me. I was envious of her ability to read

My own reading unexpectedly inspires me.

better and faster than I could; however, as long as she would read to me, I willingly overlooked that.

When I was pregnant, I remember wondering if my baby could hear all the stories I was reading and all the songs I was singing to my students at school. A few weeks after recovering from a Caesarean section and adjusting to motherhood, I once again began reading to my child. Now, Mary Chandler is 4 and in the prekindergarten classroom across the hall from mine. We are still reading together. As the teacher of 4-year-olds and the mother of a 4-year-old, I am doubly faced with literacy education every day.

Mary Chandler often tells me about books that her teacher has read during the school day: "We read *Dig a Dinosaur* [Gentner, 1993] today. Rex eats dead dinosaurs. Yuck! Did you read that book in your class today? Well you need to read it tomorrow. OK, Mom?"

My daughter loves to read, and for that I am very thankful. I only hope it will last. As I said before, I remember loving books as a child. I also remember being a struggling reader until getting reading glasses. After that, I do not have many memories about reading. There is a gap—missing pieces. I cannot put my finger on any one reason I stopped reading. I did have a few teachers who read aloud to us in elementary school. Then came boredom when reading literary classics in high school. I do not remember finishing a single book in high school. Once I was in college, I found pleasure again in reading for my literature classes, but this still was not my own reading. It was an assignment. It would seem logical to think once a reader always a reader, but that is not how it happened for me. The most important missing piece for me is reading for pleasure, simply because I wanted to read. For years, I neglected such an important part of me. I felt it was a luxury that I couldn't afford. There was simply no time to indulge in such pleasures for myself. Recently, I have reclaimed that missing piece, reading a book because I want to read it, not because I have to. I find myself taking books with me everywhere, which greatly annoys my husband; he says it is rude. I read while riding in a car and during commercial breaks while watching television.

> *I find myself taking books with me everywhere.*

As an adult, there are two experiences that I treasure most when it comes to reading. The first is reading to my daughter. I share with her words and rhythms in books such as *Oh My Baby, Little One* by Kathi Appelt (2000):

Oh my baby, little one,
The hardest thing I do
Is hold you tight, then let you go,
And walk away from you.

It slips inside your lunch box
And underneath your cap.
When your teacher reads a storybook,
It settles on your lap.

But oh my baby, little one,
The sweetest thing I do
Is sweep you up and hold you tight
And come back home to you.

The second experience first happened while my husband and I were traveling to Savannah, Georgia, for a long weekend. I had wanted to read *Midnight in the Garden of Good and Evil* by John Berendt (1994). I had seen part of the movie on television and wanted to revisit the scene of the crime, so I was sure to pick up the book a few days before our trip. I knew that I wanted to do the book tour while we were in Savannah, but I wasn't sure my husband would have the same interest. Each night, while reading the book before I went to sleep, I would inevitably feel compelled to tell my husband what was happening in the book. I knew I had hooked him when he asked me to read aloud to him in the car on our way there. I loved it. My husband reads to our daughter. He reads the newspaper and magazines and surfs the Web for information, but rarely does he pick up a book. I keep hoping to find another book that we can share together.

In examining myself as a reader, I find that these are my precious jewels: (a) being alone with the characters and feeling among friends; (b) finding the phrases, verse, and rhythms that speak to my soul; and (c) swapping titles, pointing out details, and discussing perspectives with others. Recognizing these jewels helps me know how to share reading with my daughter, my husband, and my students in ways that they, too, might find their own precious jewels as readers.

LITERATURE CITED

Appelt, K. (2000). *Oh my baby, little one.* New York: Harcourt.
Berendt, J. (1994). *Midnight in the garden of good and evil.* New York: Random House.
Gentner, N.L. (1993). *Dig a dinosaur.* Bothell, WA: The Wright Group.
Gibbons, K. (1987). *Ellen Foster.* Chapel Hill, NC: Algonquin Books.

—Barbara Robbins—
MIDDLE SCHOOL READING
AND LANGUAGE ARTS TEACHER

Barbara has taught for 25 years. She spent 12 years in DeKalb County, Georgia, teaching seventh-grade science, math, and reading, as well as gifted kindergarten through seventh grade. She also has spent 13 years in Rockdale County teaching sixth- and seventh-grade science. Currently, she is teaching academically gifted seventh- and eighth-grade reading and language arts.

Barbara felt that the seminar was the most relaxing and enjoyable class she had taken during her specialist program. She enjoyed the book club feel of the discussions, and the seminar prompted her to challenge the way her own students were expected to read. She said she hopes to bring some of the characteristics of her own enjoyment of the seminar into her classroom teaching.

Barbara's favorite reading from the Readers as Teachers and Teachers as Readers seminar was CRAZY IN ALABAMA by Mark Childress (1993). She still laughs when she thinks of some sections of the book, although other parts make her sorrowful. That book has really stayed with her.

CHAPTER 13

Freedom to Read: What Is It?

Barbara Robbins

G iving students the freedom to read. On one hand, the idea sounds almost too ridiculous to consider. Of course, we as educators strive to give our students freedom to read. We support numerous activities to promote an appreciation of reading. We provide blocks of class time to take our students to the media center. We read aloud to them in class and provide time during the school day for silent reading. Schools sponsor book fairs so students can select and purchase quality and age-appropriate literature at reduced prices. Not only do students eagerly wait to go to the book fair during a class period, but most book fairs are also open at least one evening to allow parents to get in on the spending, too. We encourage our students to read and allow them to pick which titles they buy.

On the other hand, the act of teaching children reading, or any other content area for that matter, currently allows for very little freedom of choice. A curriculum committee decides which topics will be studied in each grade. The work of the committee is then approved first by the superintendent or his or her representatives and finally by the state board of education. It is interesting that most board members are not educators. After approval of the curriculum has been given, we teachers fall into lock step and try to teach the objectives that have been mandated. Then, we monitor the reading lives of our students by having them maintain reading logs that must be validated by us and by their parents. In language arts, we give instruction on the various genres and require that our students read those genres. All this is done in an effort to instill a lifelong love of reading in our students. However, do we sometimes do more harm to our students than good? In some cases, too much structure may squelch an already developed love of reading. One component of reading instruction that educators often overlook is giving our students the freedom to read as they choose—the same freedom we, as adults, enjoy. Why can't we extend the same freedom to them that has been extended to us in the Readers as Teachers seminar? Perhaps the only requirements that should be placed on students are that (a) they *must* read something, (b) the reading must be done on a regular basis, and (c) some type of reading reflection must be written. Students should be encouraged to read magazines, newspapers, anthologies, plays, poetry, manuals, and textbooks in addition to novels. Too often, in an effort to teach reading fluency, educators inadvertently give the impression that novels are sacred texts and that any other reading material is not worthy of the time spent reading it. We must teach our students that virtually all reading has value and that there is joy to be found by reading. Educators also must teach them that reading takes place for a variety of reasons. Don't we read for a variety of purposes? Some of these purposes include to be informed, to be entertained, to appreciate the writer's craft, and to inspire ourselves as writers.

Sadly, as teachers, we often become mired in school culture, which often does away with our students' reading freedom. Examples of school culture include studying the life of Johnny Appleseed in the fall, the story of the Pilgrims and the Native Americans prior to Thanksgiving, and African American authors in February during Black History Month. Forcing students to read a variety of genres has often been part of this school culture. Too often, we have forced students to read genres in which they have absolutely no interest. It is my contention that if we want to build a community of willing child and adult readers, we must grant the gift of reading freedom at an early age, not during adulthood.

> One component of reading instruction that educators often overlook is giving our students the freedom to read as they choose.

I never entertained the idea of granting reading autonomy to my students until I was in the seminar. Even after the rationale behind our seminar and the requirements were explained, part of me was left wondering what the trick was and waiting for the real requirements to show up. For once, there was no detailed syllabus and no required reading list. I didn't have a list of assignments to complete for each class. This was definitely out of the ordinary and quite unsettling. I found it difficult to trust an authority figure who gave me permission to read whatever I wanted. After the realization that there was no trick and that all I had to do was read whatever I wanted and somehow relate my reading life experiences to my classroom, I was overwhelmed by a sense of pleasure and enjoyment. What a sense of freedom and elation this realization brought.

I am ready to share this freedom with my students. I want them to know that "reading for pleasure" is not a sly misnomer used for required reading. I want them to read whatever their hearts desire, just as I am doing now. *I want them to read.* Isn't this one of the major goals of (reading) education? Could this be a controversial idea in my gifted middle school language arts classes? You bet! Can this be an effective way to meet and satisfy the curriculum requirements that are placed on me as a teacher by my administration and county? I think so. I'm confident that I can still effectively meet all curriculum requirements. Will parents be supportive or critical of this idea? I want to find out. Will students be supportive of this idea? I'm expecting that they will be more eager to participate in this reading program rather than the one mandated by our school. Will I be challenging the canon of literature? Perhaps, because students will be choosing reading material that may not be from the traditional canon. It may also ultimately be supportive of the established canon if students choose to read literature from the canon. What I seek will be a threatening challenge to the program purchased by my media center. I am more than willing to work to show that granting my gifted students freedom to read is more beneficial and intellectually challenging than requiring them to read books simply for the sake of amassing points as they are required to do when participating in the Accelerated Reader program.

These are serious questions that require a lot of thought before I can give my students the freedom to read that I was given. Granting my students the freedom to read will definitely be contrary to the way things are done at my school. Some may say that the system we currently endorse is fine: "If it ain't broke, don't fix it." I would challenge this contention.

At my school, it seems we do something different every year. This year, every person on the faculty has to teach a reading class. Yes, everyone—from the P.E. coaches to the band directors. Needless to say, the cries of discomfort from coworkers who have never taught reading before have been loud and sustained. Lower-level reading groups use the *Read With Sarah* program, although upper-level readers use *Junior Great Books* and *Be a Better Reader* programs to try to improve test scores.

Saying that students have the freedom to read is lip service. They are free to read what they want as long as it is a novel that is written for young adults. They are free to read what they want as long as the reading material belongs to a particular reading program or is an Accelerated Reader book.

Some feel that allowing students to read below their reading level is harmful and not at all beneficial, often completely overlooking students' need or desire to revisit books for specific reasons. These reasons may include a need for comfort from a book with pleasant associations or a need to read a book written for younger audiences just for fun or because it looks appealing. Our mandated reading program requires that books be at a student's zone of proximal development. Russian psychologist Lev Vygotsky (1934/1978) was the originator of the concept of zone of proximal development. He maintained that a child follows an adult's example and develops the ability to do certain tasks without help or assistance over time. He called the difference between what a child can do with help and what he or she can do without guidance the zone of proximal development.

Many researchers and marketers have kidnapped the term *zone of proximal development* and idea and applied it to their own research. The developers of Accelerated Reader have adopted the term for their own purposes. According to Accelerated Reader literature, their use of the term means matching students to appropriate books. A student's zone of proximal development represents a level of difficulty that is neither too hard nor too easy, and it is the level at which optimal learning takes place. I would rather rely on my own knowledge of my students and texts to guide them in their independent reading.

At my school, many of the literary classics are ignored or passed over because the books don't have Accelerated Reader tests to accompany them. Sadly, accumulating Accelerated Reader points has become the most important reason to read. Several students chose not to read books I had recommended simply because it would not increase their Accelerated Reader point total. I recently recommended *My Antonia* (Cather, 1954) to a student who had come to me for book recommendations. After I told her about the basic plot and after we read the information found on the book jacket, she said it was definitely a book she would like to read, but she couldn't read it because it didn't have an Accelerated Reader test to accompany it. What a disservice to that student.

My students are free to read what they wish as long as the book contains no inappropriate language, situations, or challenges to religious teachings. These restrictions often eliminate many books written for adults or books written for adolescents, such as the books by R.L. Stine or in the Harry Potter series. Some believe that students must read only novels to be real readers, failing to recognize that the reading of magazines or newspapers is beneficial. In actuality, we do not give our students the freedom to read the material they wish to read. We control this part of their lives, as we do so many other parts.

Where does this leave me in reference to my original question, What is freedom to read? I believe that granting students the freedom to read is very important and that it should, therefore, be given to all students. Freedom to read is much more important than the accumulation of points. The majority of my gifted students are already eager and willing readers. Forcing them to read books for the sake of accumulating points in an incentive-based reading program seems counterproductive.

I presented a proposal to my principal that would allow my students to read from a variety of text sources—magazines, newspapers, poetry books, manuals—which are ignored, for the most part, by Accelerated Reader. The gifted students in my reading class would participate. They would be waived partially, if not completely, from participation in Accelerated Reader. My principal gave me the green light. My next step was an informational meeting for the parents of the students and the students themselves. The students would be required to keep extensive reading logs and write critically about what they read. Parents were asked to observe their children and write about their children's reading lives. In my plan, reading accountability was more extensive than answering the Accelerated Reader test's 10 literal questions for each book.

At first, my students felt as I did at the beginning of my seminar; they were waiting for the other shoe to drop. They were waiting for the real requirements to appear. They had many questions in the beginning and were almost fearful. I discovered that although participation in Accelerated Reader might not have been exciting, it was at least safe and comfortable for them. Granting them the freedom to read took away what was known and made them responsible for their own reading. Their new mission became reading a variety of materials, not amassing points. It was exciting to hear students discuss with their classmates and with me what they were reading. Many found a love of a genre that they never experienced before, and they wanted to explore further by reading more books in that genre. Students discovered and explored sections of our school media center that they never knew existed. They also put their parents to work by sending them to the public library on their way home from work to pick up certain titles not available in our media center. Woe to the parent who was unable to fulfill a request when expected!

Near the end of the semester, I had my students write their opinions of experiencing the freedom to read materials of their choice. There were mixed reactions. One student found the experience very different from anything she had ever done in the past, yet noted that she still did not have complete freedom to read because she was reading from genres she might not have otherwise selected.

Students discovered and explored sections of our school media center that they never knew existed.

Another student preferred participating in Accelerated Reader because she could quickly fulfill her requirements and then spend the rest of the year reading what she wanted to read. Most students wrote that they really enjoyed our reading odyssey because they were able to read from genres that were familiar, such as newspapers and magazines, that are usually overlooked by other teachers. The students responded positively to being nudged out of their comfort zones into reading from genres that were new to them *if* they liked what they read. For all my students, if they liked a text, they liked the genre. I found parents to be supportive. One reason may have been that their children did not have to be limited to reading Accelerated Reader books, which were below their children's reading level.

Despite mixed comments, I will continue to explore ways to give my students an alternative to reading for points. I continue to think that it is beneficial for students to be exposed to and read a variety of genres. I will eliminate the term *freedom to read* as the description of this undertaking because students' middle school sense of fairness was absolutely correct when they pointed out that they still did not have complete freedom to read. I was still *requiring* them to investigate various genres, prohibiting them from reading what they really wanted to read.

REFERENCE

Vygotsky, L.S. (1978). *Mind in society: The development of higher psychological processes.* Cambridge, MA: Harvard University Press. (Original work published in 1934)

LITERATURE CITED

Cather, W. (1954). *My Antonia.* Boston: Houghton Mifflin.
Childress, M. (1993). *Crazy in Alabama.* New York: Putnam.

—Tricia Bridges—
SECOND-GRADE TEACHER

Tricia began her career at the Washington Wilkes Primary School in Washington, Georgia, as a long-term substitute in the media center. She is currently in her 10th year as a second-grade teacher there. She has also been a history teacher in Louisiana, and her career has been punctuated by many moves as a military wife.

Tricia's favorite readings during the Readers as Teachers and Teachers as Readers seminar were books by the authors Nicholas Sparks and Lori Wick. Sparks puts "sparks in your heart" as one reads his novels. His messages often could be related to the reader's own personal life, and his books have a way of reaching, teaching, and helping readers such as Tricia stay attuned to their feelings about life and the many ways one may handle life's conflicts. As an author, Wick seems deeply involved in religion. She uses this interest to share deep messages with her readers, without being a fanatic about religion. She uses her faith in her stories and makes her readers think about everlasting life and the warmth that comes from knowing about it. Tricia recommends books by both of these authors for others to read.

Tricia would like to thank her friend and former colleague Carolyn Gammon for her help, support, and time while she prepared her essay.

CHAPTER 14

Reading Is an Adventure You Don't Want to Miss

Tricia Bridges

I remember always having a love for reading. As a child, I always had a book with me when my family traveled somewhere, even if it was just on a short trip. I have never been able just to sit and do nothing. I have long considered reading as a way to relax, especially as I've gotten older and have acquired more responsibilities. My husband always says, "Oh, that must be a good book," or "I see you started another book." I am one of those people who has a book with me all the time. If I go fishing with my family, I have a book tucked away somewhere. If I go on a trip, I have a book. I always am prepared just in case I have to wait on something or somebody. Through the various genres of what I read or have read, I find that I can often use my readings as problem solvers. Reading sometimes helps me to understand more of the problems my students go through, and it makes me feel better equipped to help them. My mom and sister both love to read, so when I go to their houses for the weekend, we love to sit together and read. What a great way to relax after a hectic week of teaching!

Reading is such a wonderful experience to do alone or to share with someone you want to see enjoy reading as much as you do. I want to be able to help my students become better readers, and I feel that if I show my enthusiasm for reading, they will become more enthusiastic. While reading in the classroom, I try to make books as interesting to my class as I can. I am open and willing to hear my students' interpretations of what we read. I want students to be able to read words and ponder how those words might matter to them. I relate my reading experiences and try to relate those of others; I can demonstrate a love for reading. My hope is that my students will be on their way to becoming lifelong readers, which in turn will lead them to become lifelong learners.

On the first night of the Readers as Teachers and Teachers as Readers seminar, I became very excited during the discussion of the course and its requirements. As I sat and listened, I realized I needed to pay a visit to the personal library of my friend and former colleague, Carolyn. My mind wandered to something Carolyn always said: "Reading is an adventure you don't want to miss." I pulled my thoughts back to the present; I couldn't help but think, What a great class for a person who loves reading as much as I do.

I want students to be able to read words and ponder how those words might matter to them.

While I still had all these wonderful thoughts roaming around in my head, I called my reading friend, Carolyn. I started with my immediate need, books to read. My seminar required I read and read anything. While teaching with Carolyn for eight years, one of the things I learned was that we shared a love for reading. When I would say, "Carolyn, I need something to read," she immediately would have a great book in mind and bring it the next day. I learned to trust her judgment in bringing me books; we shared the same interest in them. Before the seminar, I had never seen her library at home. I was honored to enter that room. It was like a bookstore where the only payment was sharing the love of reading.

There were rows and rows of books. On one side of the room, I saw a computer with various things lying around on the table. About five bookcases lined the walls of the room. Research books were hidden behind the doors of one bookcase, inspirational books in another area, and then a whole shelf of craft books. Who could miss the shelves containing wonderful children's literature that Carolyn so lovingly used during her years of teaching? The other books were arranged in alphabetical order by author. She had 425 novels alone in that one room! Carolyn even had lots of her childhood books and was quick to let me know that they were antiques. I saw book after book that I wanted to read. I don't know how long I looked, but I had a wonderful time browsing through books that I would eventually borrow.

Carolyn and I looked at the list of books I had written down during my seminar as other teachers shared their reading choices. I told Carolyn of my joy in having a class in which I could read what I wanted and not feel guilty about which book it was or how long it took to read. I was free to say to my family, "I am doing the work my professor requires." Together, Carolyn and I found books on the list, but as we talked about what I wanted to read, she began pulling out books she knew I would enjoy. On my own, I usually read a lot of books that don't require a whole lot of thinking but are just fun to read and relax with. I wanted to use this seminar opportunity to read books I may not have typically chosen. I found that I wanted to broaden my horizons and try new books.

Carolyn handed me book after book until I said, "Stop." She was excited to tell me about the books. I was amazed that she remembered so much about them. I left with about 12 books, but before I left, Carolyn even helped prioritize my reading. She said, "You will love them all, but read them in this order." She told me to read *The Guardian* by Dee Henderson (2001), *A Walk to Remember* by Nicholas Sparks (2000), and *Sophie's Heart* by Lori Wick (1995). After those, I should read *Wish You Well* by David Baldacci (2001), *A Painted House* by John Grisham (2001), *1st to Die: A Novel* by James Patterson (2001), and *The Last Time They Met* by Anita Shreve (2001). Carolyn assured me there was no hurry to return them. She was such a generous person to share her books with me, but I know I am not the only one who benefits. She loves to read and wants to instill that love for reading in others. Maybe I will read something new and suggest she add it to her library.

When I told my students about Carolyn, and all the books she owned, they were so interested that I decided to find out more about Carolyn. I gave her a call to set up an interview to discuss further her love of reading and how it has shaped her life. The interview began with questions about her background. Carolyn had just recently retired after 33 years of teaching. Thirty of those years were spent at Washington Wilkes Primary School, and all were in second grade. When I asked about how she became a teacher, Carolyn said, "If you want to have fun, fun, fun for the rest of your life, become a teacher!" She went on to tell me that with any other job, she would have gotten bored. Carolyn feels that one needs to be a little antsy and imaginative and definitely have a sense of humor to become a teacher of small children. Well, Carolyn certainly has these qualities. She had many honors bestowed on her while teaching, and since I've been at Washington Wilkes, I can only remember one day that she was absent from school. Carolyn felt that her childhood and adolescent years led her to the inevitable—being a teacher. What a great role model for me and for any child!

Next, I asked Carolyn about her childhood reading. I asked her if anyone read to her, what her favorite books were, and if she could just share a few memories of her childhood. Carolyn's recollections of her childhood reading were much more vivid than my own. Carolyn told me that her parents were hard-working farmers who usually didn't have the time to read to her. She wanted to emphasize that many boys and girls today are very fortunate to have parents with time to read to them. Carolyn said she always has enjoyed reading, but she isn't sure how that love started. She feels a thirst for the literature. Carolyn said, "When I was in fifth grade, one of my favorite teachers gave me some of her personal books to take home to read because I didn't have any books at home. My parents were not able to afford them." In the first and second grades, Carolyn's favorites were the Bobbsey Twins books. She said she graduated to Nancy Drew books and *Little Women* (Alcott, 1869/1997).

Carolyn shared that when she was little she used to love to read so much that at night she would get a flashlight and read under the covers in bed so her parents wouldn't see the light on in her room. "If you can read, you can travel anywhere in the world and experience anything," Carolyn said. Like me, Carolyn says she is in her own little world while she is reading.

When I asked Carolyn if she ever experienced any problems when learning to read she said, "I was very fortunate; it just came naturally." I asked if after all her years of teaching she had any tips for those struggling readers. She replied, "The best thing to do is listen to other people read and hear how the inflection in their voices communicates meaning. Listening to others read helps children experience going places, even if they are struggling with their own reading." Carolyn added, "If you enjoy reading, you can learn to read. It just sort of soaks in most of the time."

Carolyn considers herself a well-rounded reader. She reads for pleasure and professional reasons, even though she's retired. Carolyn reads professional magazines to help other teachers, including her daughter-in-law. Some magazines she enjoys reading are *Instructor, The Reading Teacher, School Days, Good Apple Magazine*, and *P.A.G.E. Journal*. Carolyn is always reaching out for new ideas and searching for something new and different to pass along.

When asked how often she reads, Carolyn told me she could read all day long and has been known to read all night long, not even realizing the time. Even while substitute teaching, which she occasionally does, Carolyn said she still tries to get in an hour of reading every day.

Carolyn and I talked about a project I had in mind for my classroom. I wanted people from different walks of life to visit my class so my students could interview them about their love for reading and how learning to read has been important in their lives. A starting point for my students would be my interview with Carolyn as an example. After the interview, she would read to us. Then, I hoped the children would think of who is important in their reading lives. I would like to have my students write letters to those individuals and ask them questions. Then we could invite each of those people to come to our classroom for an interview and to read a favorite story.

"[I]n every walk of life, reading is important."

Despite their differences and unique needs, I want all my students to feel that they have something to contribute to this project. Students would be fulfilling many objectives throughout this project. They would be acquiring letter-writing skills and communication skills as they invite others to our classroom. I would let each child nominate someone who she feels is important to the shaping of her own reading. I would draw a name out each week, and I would help that child with her letter writing and questions, if needed. I hope I would begin to see a difference in the type of literature the children are choosing from the media center. Finally, through our visits and the children's questions to our visitors, I hope I would observe a growth in my students' lives as they experience the adventure of reading in their own lives and that of others.

In my last interview question for Carolyn, I asked her why she considers reading important while a person is young as opposed to later in life. She said, "When you are in second grade, you don't know your future, but in every walk of life, reading is important. You need to learn to read for any type of job you have, and you need to learn to read for pleasure. Any given time of the day you are going to need to read. Everywhere you go, there is an adventure in reading, an adventure you don't want to miss!"

LITERATURE CITED

Alcott, L.M. (1997). *Little women*. New York: Puffin. (Original work published 1869)

Baldacci, D. (2001). *Wish you well*. New York: Warner Books.

Grisham, J. (2001). *A painted house*. New York: Island Books.

Henderson, D. (2001). *The guardian*. Sisters, OR: Multnomah.

Patterson, J. (2001). *1st to die: A novel*. Boston: Little, Brown.

Shreve, A. (2001). *The last time they met*. Boston: Little, Brown.

Sparks, N. (2000). *A walk to remember*. New York: Warner Books.

Wick, L. (1995). *Sophie's heart*. Eugene, OR: Harvest House.

—Debbie Barrett—
MIDDLE SCHOOL LANGUAGE ARTS TEACHER

Debbie has taught language arts for 11 years. Before her children were born, she taught music for 3 years. She received her master's degree in middle school education from the University of Georgia in 1995. When Debbie was teaching seventh- and eighth-grade language arts, she realized she missed the camaraderie she had felt with other language arts and reading teachers when enrolled in her master's degree program. Therefore, she began a program for a specialist's degree in language education and hopes to finish in the spring of 2003.

The Readers as Teachers and Teachers as Readers seminar felt to Debbie as if she had finally reached the dessert course of a meal! To be able to read books she wanted to read and listen to others talk about books they had read was a treat. Her favorite reading selection was MISS JULIA SPEAKS HER MIND: A NOVEL by Ann B. Ross (2000). Debbie loved the humor of Miss Julia, the proper Southern woman who is widowed and childless and yet suddenly is left with her deceased husband's illegitimate child.

Debbie also has learned to appreciate the wisdom she finds in books, such as in Joyce Rockwood's TO SPOIL THE SUN (1987) when one of the Native Americans states,

> We walk a path of constant changing. With each change there is a sadness for what we have lost and a confusion about what we have become. It happens to us again and again, and each time we are caught by surprise and do not recognize at first what has happened, because always we think we have already changed for the last time. But there is no last time. (p. 76)

Debbie could relate to this excerpt because she felt changed by the seminar in unexpected ways.

CHAPTER 15

Reading Can Create Lines of Communication

Debbie Barrett

Dear Laura Leigh (Barrett),

You may not be aware of the tremendous influence you have had in my life, but I'm writing to thank you for sparking my interest in reading for pleasure. It has transformed my life. Now all I want to do in my spare time is read! I look forward to sharing titles and tidbits of stories with you. Without your knowing it, you gave me one of the best gifts ever.

Love,
Mom

even years ago, my daughter Laura Leigh was 12 years old. She read books constantly, especially Mary Higgins Clark mysteries. I overheard conversations between Laura Leigh and her grandmother, "Who do you think is the murderer in *All Around the Town* (1992)?" "I'm reading *Remember Me* (1994) next." Slowly, like the warmth of a fire permeating a cold room, the desire to read those fictional books from which my daughter just could not tear herself away crept into my world. Laura Leigh started enticing me, "Mom, you really need to read this one. It's so good!" I was hooked. Seven years later, the teacher part of me wants this moment to occur in another parent's life.

It is interesting to think about how I've learned from my daughter. I remember my daughter's reading during her stormy high school years. It was the fine thread that kept us connected when our worlds seemed to rotate in different universes. I mentioned this one evening in the Readers as Teachers and Teachers as Readers seminar. The teachers asked if I ever had my seventh-grade students write letters to their parents about what they were reading. Perhaps, they suggested, I would find my students and their parents connecting through reading much as I had with my daughter. It had not occurred to me, but now it seems odd because I know from experience that reading can be a means of keeping the lines of communication open between parent and child, especially in the teenage years when the adolescent can be unpredictable and questioning.

I saw the possibility for adding this student-parent connection to my class literature circles. At the beginning of the year, I presented the idea of literature circles in hopes that students would look forward to sharing experiences and would personally recognize the value of the written word. My seventh graders seemed ready for the opportunity. Enthusiastically, they asked, "Can we choose our own groups? Can we choose what books to read?" I was extremely pleased that literature circles had been so welcomed. With equal enthusiasm, we set about choosing books for each group to read and organizing the students into circles of three or four students. We spent weeks reading, sharing, and connecting with one another.

Our culminating project would be writing a letter to parents (or older family members). Each student would write about something significant to him or her about the book, and the family member would be invited to write a letter in reply to the student. Complaints were hurled forth. Questions were thrown like daggers: "Do we have to write our parents?" "What if my parent won't write me back? Does that affect my grade?" "Why can't we write a friend?" "What will I say to my mom about my book?" I had no idea the response would be so negative from my students who had been such a cheering crowd for the literature circles. Obviously, I had touched a nerve, which made me wonder, Why are these students so anxious about writing a letter to their parents?

My curiosity was intense. I waited and anticipated these letters that would inform the parent about the child's most favorite and least favorite parts of the book, as well as how the student had connected personally with the text. Even more eagerly, I anticipated the parents' responses. Part of me worried, even though I would not and did not admit it to my students. I secretly thought half the students would come to class saying, "I don't have a letter" or "My mom didn't have time to write a letter."

The due date arrived; the students eagerly took their seats and were calling out questions as they came in, "Can we share our letters? Can I read my letter from my mom?" What a Jekyll and Hyde difference from only two days before! Had someone kidnapped my class? Because this was the first time I had attempted such an assignment, I asked for volunteers to read their letters as well as those from their parents. I was amazed!

Some letters simply affirmed the parents' feelings for their children, such as the one from John's mom:

> Dear Son,
>
> It's so nice of you to write me a letter. The book that you just finished sounds real interesting. I am proud to know that you would change the bad part to do a good thing. I enjoy writing to you; maybe we can start doing it more often. Always remember that I love you and I am always here if you need me.
>
> Love,
> Mom

One mother emphasized her dislike of guns after reading her son's letter about *Incident at Hawk's Hill* (Eckert, 1971): "George Burton [a character in the book] sounds terrible. See why I hate guns so much? Crazy people like him can kill too easily. Or not crazy people...."

I read in these letters how parents could aid in extending the child's thinking or offer a challenge about the reading material. After Ashley read *Scorpions* (Myers, 1988) and wrote to her mom, the mother replied, "This story teaches you to have more respect for others, take responsibility, and be more caring." Encouragement from parents was evident. Mick's mother and father responded to their son's letter about *Scorpions* with a hopeful voice:

> The events you described sound action packed. What other issues did the characters face? Were they able to resolve the

conflicts without more violence? You are correct that the
events in the story do happen in real life. It is sad that so
many young teenagers (and even younger children) have to
deal with gang issues and try to stay safe each day. Each day
we pray that you will be strong in the face of such issues and
continue to make good decisions in your own life.

Love,
Your Parents (Mama & Dad)

Melissa's mom also was encouraging:

My dearest Melissa,

Thank you so much for the letter; I was very much surprised. I
am doing fine and was glad to hear about the book you are
reading. Your comprehension skills are growing, and you are
a very smart young lady. I will be watching for more signs of
your growth in your studies as the year goes on. I am very
proud of you, and you should be proud of yourself.

Keep studying,
Mom

Another parent affirmed how books can sometimes teach
values. In response to her daughter's letter about *Scorpions*, the
mother penned,

The book dealt with a situation about a brother having to do
the unthinkable (sell crack) to pay for his brother's appeal. I
think there is a valuable lesson for all kids and my daughter in
this book. My daughter really enjoyed reading this book. She
talks about *Scorpions* frequently. These are the types of
books that really spark her desire to read and learn new
things. Thanks.

I believe parents value reading. I believe parents care about
what happens in their children's classrooms and want to maintain
good communication with their adolescent children. The letter-
response assignment confirmed my beliefs. There are still more
positives to be explored using this new communication through
books. Both parent and child could share experiences relating to

how each personally connected with the text. Controversies about issues in the book might arise, which would be an opportune setting for sharing opinions and beliefs, perhaps, about teenage issues such as alcohol, drug abuse, guns, sex, shoplifting, or peer pressure. Each participant would agree ahead of time to agree or disagree and still be respectful of the other's thoughts. This interaction might even be a subtle way for a parent to advise.

More questions about future opportunities surfaced as I wondered, What if I had parent and child read the same book and share discussions or journal responses? How would the child feel sharing with a parent what he or she has read if it's a touchy issue? Could this hurt a parent-child relationship? Or, could the book, perhaps, bridge the gap about a particular issue between the parent and the child? What if the parent is not a lifelong reader and the child spurs his parent to read? That thought once again triggered memories of my own reading with my daughter. How can I continue to foster this cross-generational communication? In the literature circles, I had chosen approximately seven books for the students to vote on by secret ballot. How would the books be chosen now? Would the student or parent choose the book, or would they both choose one together? The parent-child reading interactions would have to be documented somehow. Multiple documentation avenues could be used—interview between parent and child, journals, taped conversations, letters, or diaries. Parents could even be participants in the discussions in the literature circles. There's so much to consider.

> Through communicating about books, parents can truly learn their children's needs, desires, and concerns.

Young people want to be listened to; they want their ideas to be heard. In her book *In the Middle: New Understandings About Reading, Writing, and Learning*, Nancie Atwell (1998) advises that students as writers need response while their words are still churning. Why not offer a parent's genuine response to a child's thoughts, ideas, and perspectives while the clay is still malleable? Through communicating about books, parents can truly learn their children's needs, desires, and concerns, and consequently, nurture the parent-child relationship even more. And who knows? Another spark may ignite and create a new lifelong reader like me!

Dear Laura Leigh,

Seven years have passed since you sparked my interest in reading. My reading for pleasure has grown during those years, and now you're in college. It's amazing that we're still sharing book ideas with each other. Our discussions about your freshman English course authors and essays have enlightened me as well as kept me in touch with you in your new world. I look forward to this summer when we can work on crossword puzzles together again as well as share books.

Love you,
Mom

REFERENCE

Atwell, N. (1998) *In the middle: New understandings about reading, writing, and learning.* Portsmouth, NH: Boynton/Cook.

LITERATURE CITED

Clark, M.H. (1992). *All around the town.* New York: Simon & Schuster.
Clark, M.H. (1994). *Remember me.* New York: Simon & Schuster.
Eckert, A.W. (1971). *Incident at Hawk's Hill.* Boston: Little, Brown.
Myers, W.D. (1988). *Scorpions.* New York: HarperCollins.
Rockwood, J. (1987). *To spoil the sun.* New York: Henry Holt.
Ross, A.B. (2000). *Miss Julia speaks her mind: A novel.* New York: Harper.

—Vicki Gina Hanson—
EARLY INTERVENTION PROGRAM TEACHER

Vicki is in the middle of her third year of teaching. She has taught at Maysville Elementary in Maysville, Georgia, for all three years. For the first two years, she taught early intervention program (EIP) reading to first and second graders in small groups. Vicki is still an EIP teacher, but she is teaching reading to kindergarten through fifth grades in small groups as well.

In her childhood and teens, Vicki was an avid reader and sometimes found it difficult to juggle the time spent with work and the time spent curled up with a good book. By examining the importance of reading for enjoyment as an adult, Vicki is now much more aware of and able to fight the time constraints at school and make reading a priority. Since the seminar, Vicki is much more aware of how important it is for a teacher to be a reader as well. When she hit reality without the support of the seminar participants, teaching—the job she loves—took over again.

Vicki's favorite reading during the seminar was LOST LAYSEN by Margaret Mitchell (1997). She read it in one day, in fact. Not only was it exciting to find another book by the author of GONE WITH THE WIND (1937/1996), but the history behind the new book also was enticing to her as a reader. By reading the foreword of LOST LAYSEN, Vicki found out that Mitchell had requested that all her manuscripts be destroyed in the event of her death. Mitchell wrote the story and gave it to one of her beaus; a family member of the beau found it years later. The fact that the tale, a tragic love story, was given to Mitchell's beau interested Vicki. LOST LAYSEN also includes photographs of Mitchell's life and times, which really added to Vicki's enjoyment of the book.

CHAPTER 16

My Reading Journey: From Child to Teacher

Vicki Gina Hanson

"T was the night before Christmas, and all through the house, not a creature was stirring, not even a mouse…" (Moore, 1823/2002, p. 1). My mother tells of many nights that I chose this book and "read" with her, having memorized the print on the page. I remember being totally taken with the pictures and imagined myself watching Santa's belly shake like a bowl full of jelly. I even went so far as to "see" Santa one Christmas Eve in my living room!

When thinking of my own childhood reading, I also remember an obscure book titled *You're Going out There a Kid, but You're Coming Back a Star* (Wallner, 1984), a story about the troubles of a preteen girl who desperately wants to be older. When I came home from school, having just found out that the boy I had a crush on liked someone else, I curled up with this book and shared my tragedy with the main character. Somehow, I didn't seem so alone anymore.

Books have generated lifelong curiosities for me. My fascination with historical fiction, especially about pioneer times, began with *Little House on the Prairie* (Wilder, 1953). I can remember the joy that bubbled up in me when I found *On the Way Home: The Diary of a Trip From South Dakota to Mansfield, Missouri, 1894* (Lane, 1962) and *West From Home: Letters of Laura Ingalls Wilder, San Francisco, 1915* (MacBride, 1994). Because of the Little House books, some of my favorite authors today, Lori Wick and Francine Rivers to name a couple, are ones who also have written of pioneer times.

Books often have given me confidence. When I heard my parents arguing, when I was going through middle school misery, and when I went away to college, I immersed myself in my favorites. I mentally walked with Anne Shirley by a lake of shining waters (Montgomery, 1998) in much the same way as I now mentally ride in the covered wagons of the women in Jane Kirkpatrick's novel *All Together in One Place: A Novel of Kinship, Courage, and Faith* (2000) when I want to escape from everyday life.

Imagine me, this girl who has always been a lover of books and the stories that they painted in my imagination, actually getting to teach reading, my favorite thing, all day, every day to first and second graders. This job, which I consider a blessing, also carries with it the responsibility to be a person who opens up the world by opening books and inviting students to travel the pages of print and experience new people, places, and events.

As an EIP teacher in a school that is filled with students who aren't living the lighthearted life that we think of as childhood, I encounter students who struggle with neglect, hopelessness, and the worries of adulthood. I want to be able to show the students how much joy is in the world by offering them the companionship of books.

> This job, which I consider a blessing, also carries with it the responsibility to be a person who opens up the world by opening books.

As teachers, we often feel so bound by curriculum and the correct way to teach that we don't sit down and think about what is really best for each of our students and their development as people who live in the world with us. As a third-year teacher, I think back on my anticipation and nervousness about my first year of teaching. I was just out of college and determined to follow the manuals and programs that I was given. I am sure that the students grew as readers, but as I think back on that year, I remember how I felt guilty pulling a book off the shelves and reading to the students just for fun at the end of each period. I am thankful that my desire to convey to my students my love of reading and to foster this love is overcoming the guilt. I would and still do read to the students from *The Twits* (Dahl,

1998), *Piggie Pie* (Palatini, 1997), and *The True Story of the Three Little Pigs by A. Wolf* (Scieszka, 1995) just for fun, just for the pure enjoyment of escaping for a few moments into another world. That first year, when I made sure that we made time to read for fun, the students immediately responded by asking "May I pick a book for you to read?" and "Can you read it again, Ms. Hanson?" I even remember reading *The Twits* to one group of second graders, and one student saying, "You sound just like Mrs. Twit, Ms. Hanson." That was exciting for me. The students were into the story, relating to the characters and learning. Some students had been so bogged down in decoding, spelling, and handwriting that they did not care one way or the other about reading.

After I examined my own reading life, I noticed that I love to read books over and over. Why shouldn't my students want the same? I have students who now regularly check out extra books from me to take home, often the same books over and over, such as *Dogzilla* (1993a) and *Kat Kong* (1993b) by Dave Pilkey. These are not the books that they take home for homework and are supposed to share with me the next day. Their choices are books that shine with the glow of story lovers' hands, whose pages are tattered and creased by little fingers searching for excitement, escape, and relief. As I look at the reading program we are using at my school, I have concluded that overall it is a good program. But why do we leave out more personal and powerful reasons to read, such as reading for the pure pleasure of it?

> [W]hy do we leave out more personal and powerful reasons to read, such as reading for the pure pleasure of it?

LITERATURE CITED

Dahl, R. (1998). *The Twits*. New York: Puffin.

Kirkpatrick, J. (2000). *All together in one place: A novel of kinship, courage, and faith*. Colorado Springs, CO: Waterbrook Press.

Lane, R.W. (Ed.). (1962). *On the way home: The diary of a trip from South Dakota to Mansfield, Missouri, 1894*. New York: HarperCollins.

MacBride, R.L. (Ed.). (1994). *West from home: Letters of Laura Ingalls Wilder, San Francisco, 1915*. New York: HarperTrophy.

Mitchell, M. (1996). *Gone with the wind*. New York: Scribner. (Original work published 1937)

Mitchell, M. (1997). *Lost Laysen*. New York: Scribner.

Montgomery, L.M. (1998). *Anne of Green Gables*. New York: Gramercy.

Moore, C.C. (2002). *Twas the night before Christmas, or account of a visit from St. Nicholas*. Cambridge, MA: Candlewick. (Original work published 1823)

Palatini, M. (1997). *Piggie pie*. New York: Houghton Mifflin.

Pilkey, D. (1993a). *Dogzilla*. New York: Harcourt.

Pilkey, D. (1993b). *Kat Kong*. New York: Harcourt.

Scieszka, J. (1995). *The true story of the three little pigs by A. Wolf*. New York: Dutton.

Wallner, J. (1984). *You're going out there a kid, but you're coming back a star*. New York: Bantam.

Wilder, L.I. (1953). *Little house on the prairie*. New York: HarperTrophy.

—Annette Santana—
TEACHER EDUCATOR

Annette has been a classroom teacher for six years, teaching in a variety of classrooms from prekindergarten to fourth grade. She taught children's literature and language arts methods classes to preservice teachers at the University of Georgia for two years while she worked on her doctorate. During the course of the seminar, Annette decided to go back to teaching in the elementary classroom. Her love of books and sharing of that love were evident in her discussions and in her commitment to return to the classroom.

Annette's favorite reading from the Readers as Teachers and Teachers as Readers seminar was MEMOIRS OF A BOOKBAT by Katheryn Lasky (1994) because it highlights what Annette wants to share as a teacher— the books she reads, what she loves about them, and how those two things connect.

CHAPTER 17

Dear Teacher:
You See I Love to Read
Annette Santana

*D*ear teacher colleagues,
I need your help. Help me think through this. You see, I love to read. I cannot remember a time when reading was not a regular part of my daily life. Now that I am a teacher, this love has grown to include a love of teaching reading. This love came later in life, however, and did not guarantee I could teach reading well. Initially, I think I taught reading badly, and I recognized this flaw in every student I lost to the water fountain, the bathroom, or to pencils they sharpened into 2-inch distractions during our designated reading time. Now, I'm trying to discover what I love about reading and figure out how to share what I consider to be an emotional and intellectual advantage.

As a reader, I spend time building my power of understanding. Sometimes, I think reading resembles a fast-paced search for facts or important information that I might want to ponder. Other times, reading happens slowly so I can form pictures in my mind of what the people or places I am reading about look like, at least in my opinion. Reading happens naturally in different ways and for different reasons. Reading holds power with every word that becomes a picture in a reader's head or a morsel in a person's soul. I try to remember this along with the wisdom of Mark Twain who wrote, "The [person] who does not read good books has no advantage over the [person] who cannot read them."

Once, while observing a student teacher, I heard a classroom of fourth-grade students proclaim the injustice tied to Grace's story in Mary Hoffman's 1991 picture book, *Amazing Grace*. Grace's class play, *Peter Pan*, could not have a black girl as the lead—at least in the mind of her classmates. Students listening to this story expressed outrage, and the discussion that ensued about prejudice and what students could accomplish regardless of ethnicity represented what appreciating and understanding reading is all about. Stealing this moment of intense emotion and intellectual awakening from the students to create a story map or a sequence of events might have buried the message Hoffman so eloquently crafts and passionately shares with children.

> *Reading holds power with every word that becomes a picture in a reader's head or a morsel in a person's soul.*

Meaning from reading comes from the relevance of the words and the power of the verbal pictures or information crafted by the author for our knowledge and enjoyment. I, as a teacher and an experienced reader, realize my students may not always be supported to decipher, decode, or even appreciate the reading put before them. So is my primary job breaking down text into a skills-based learning experience so students can work toward this higher level of reading enjoyment later in their school experience, say, maybe in college? This logic appears to represent a major belief of many curriculum directors and policymakers who seem to applaud and push skills-based curricula. This acclaim is, however, only partially accurate. True, skills and tools remain necessary parts of becoming a reader, but they do not and cannot stand alone at any grade or age level.

When struggling readers find the key to decoding words, they enjoy the amazement of finally understanding reading—not standards or comprehension questions but words strung together in meaningful ways. In Patricia Polacco's book *Thank You, Mr. Falker* (1998), the main character has problems learning to read because of dyslexia; sounding out has never worked for her. Finally, after months of working with a reading teacher, as well as Mr. Falker, the true meaning behind reading comes to the girl. Mr. Falker puts a book in front of her that she's never seen before. He picks a paragraph in the middle of the page and points at it. Almost as if it were magic, or as if light poured into her brain, the words and sentences start to take shape on the page as they never have before. "She...marched...them...off...to..." (n.p.). Slowly, she reads a sentence. Then another and another. And finally she's read a paragraph. And she understands the whole thing.

So now I ask you, isn't understanding the primary goal in reading? Isn't each person's understanding as individual as the person is? We read to make meaning. Think of your students as I think of mine. Are they struggling to answer someone else's comprehension questions or to define vocabulary words someone else decided were important? Or, is the struggle their attempt to *understand* what they are reading? Most students rush to find answers to programmed assignments and are never ready for self-selected reading time to be over. Learning skills in reading remains a crucial and an ongoing part of reading, but this is not the ultimate goal in my teaching. What about other teachers? I wonder. I know, as a reader, I would lose the power and pleasure in my reading if every step I took into a book, magazine, or newspaper was mired in searching for answers to someone else's questions.

I think of Scout's introduction to reading class in *To Kill a Mockingbird* (Lee, 1960):

> She [the teacher] discovered that I was literate and looked at me with more than faint distaste. Miss Caroline told me to tell my father not to teach me anymore. It would interfere with my reading. Until I feared I would lose it, I never loved to read. One does not love breathing. (p. 18)

What have you read lately? Was it a meaningful experience? If so, was it meaningful because you had a discussion with a friend after you read it? Was it meaningful because you were reminded of a similar family situation that made you cry from laughter or sadness? I doubt the meaning came from learning a new word or remembering the order of events, don't you? I know meaning does not come to me in these ways.

In *Memoirs of a Bookbat* by Kathryn Lasky (1994), the main character, Harper, shares her way of reading:

> Just that afternoon at the library story time, Nancy had read a beautiful poem about a baby bat being born soaring and swooping through the night, skimming across treetops to find

my way through the dense forest in the darkest night. I listen to the shining needle points of sound in every book. I read. I am no bookworm. I am the bookbat. (p. 32)

The poem describes bats' sharp ears, sharp teeth, and their quick, sharp faces. It tells how they soar and loop through the night, how they listen by sending out what the poet calls "shining needle points of sound" (p. 32). The poet remarks, "Bats live by hearing. I realized...right then, that when I read I am like a bat" (p. 31).

So, dear teacher colleagues, we have a lot in common, you and I. We chose to be teachers. This choice automatically creates a multitude of daily realities we both experience—a set of standards to guide our teaching, the ever-pressing issue of grading and deciding the quality of students' work, and teaching reading, to name a few. My goal is to share my reading life with my students—what I read, what I love about it, and how these connect. I believe that before students can become engaged readers they have to see others, people like you and me, people they respect and admire, enjoying the experience of reading. Students who see tears, laughter, and satisfaction packed in a book may then desire to discover the same experiences for themselves. Do you agree?

> *I believe that before students can become engaged readers they have to see others...enjoying the experience of reading.*

LITERATURE CITED

Hoffman, M. (1991). *Amazing Grace*. New York: Dial.
Lasky, K. (1994). *Memoirs of a bookbat*. San Diego: Harcourt.
Lee, H. (1960). *To kill a mockingbird*. New York: Warner Books.
Polacco, P. (1998). *Thank you, Mr. Falker*. New York: Philomel.

CHAPTER 18

All Together Now: Proposing Stances for Teachers as Readers

Michelle Commeyras, Betty Shockley Bisplinghoff, and Jennifer Olson

T he International Reading Association's position statement on *Excellent Reading Teachers* (2000) names six critical qualities of the teachers' knowledge and practice:

1. They understand reading and writing development, and believe all children can learn to read and write.

2. They continually assess children's individual reading progress and relate reading instruction to children's previous experiences.

3. They know a variety of ways to teach reading, when to use each method, and how to combine the methods into an effective instructional program.

4. They offer a variety of materials and texts for children to read.

5. They use flexible grouping strategies to tailor instruction to individual students.

6. They are good reading "coaches" (that is, they provide help strategically). (n.p.)

Our Readers as Teachers and Teachers as Readers collaborative experience leads us (18 teachers) to propose additional qualities that may matter with regard to what teachers bring with them to class—how they pack their book bags, so to speak.

Those who joined the seminar did so because they longed for a sanctioned time for reading whatever they wanted to read. The seminar was a first-time offering. Never before had teachers at the University of Georgia been able to take a course that counted toward a graduate degree that allowed them to read whatever they chose. It seemed too good to be true. At the first seminar meeting, the teachers said they were waiting for a list of required academic texts on teachers as readers to surface. At the end of the first three hours of talk about what we had read recently or what we were currently reading, someone asked what the required reading was for the next week. When Michelle said that it was up to each person to find what she wanted to read, there was a moment of silence, as if everyone were trying to finally absorb the potential and responsibility of this real freedom to read.

After all our seminar discussions and after writing essays and reading and revising them, we feel bold enough to recommend an addition to the Association's statement that "excellent reading teachers share many of the characteristics of good teachers in general" (n.p.). We think excellent reading teachers share many of the characteristics of good *readers* in general. Good readers possess positive habits and attitudes about reading. They focus on the meaning of what they read using a variety of strategies, including considering any background knowledge that seems relevant. Good readers tend to read a variety of texts according to their specific individual needs. It seems obvious to us that excellent teachers of reading bring their reading lives to the teaching of reading and language arts. We want to challenge the divide between who we are as readers and who we are as teachers. Each must inform the other, and through this enhanced literate living, professional development becomes more organic. In addition, we propose that the language of standards for reading and language arts needs to incorporate the concept of stances. Standards refer to a level of quality or excellence desired or attained, whereas stances refer to attitudes or views that people take about something. In studying ourselves as readers who teach and teachers who read, we have realized how the stances we take toward the habits of reading enhance our efforts to meet educational standards with our students.

What we find lacking in the current concern with standards is the potential significance of the teacher coming out to his or her students as a reader. Perhaps this is because there is no research that shows a direct relationship between teachers sharing their reading lives with students and students' performances on achievement tests. The essays in this book explore the potential of a teacher's personal reading to enrich teaching in general and teaching reading and language arts specifically. Does this matter in regard to children's achievement on reading tests? We do not have the kind of scientific evidence that is being called for by the No Child Left Behind legislation. What we do have is confirmation that our students appreciate and respond to knowing us as readers. We think developing genuine reciprocal reading relationships with students around reading may be far more significant and long lasting in regard to quality of life than reading performance reported through test scores.

On December 4, 2001, we readers who teach gathered for the last time. We spent our three hours together considering what we had learned from our shared inquiry as readers who teach and teachers who read. Below are the stances we identified as important in striving to meet both teacher and student standards. We selected a few examples from our transcripts and essays to help illustrate the need for adding new stances to the more rehearsed concept of standards. We hope that other teachers find these stances compelling enough to bring their reading selves into their classrooms.

1. Teachers as Readers Let Their Students See Them Reading a Variety of Texts

It sounds so simple. Drop everything and read (DEAR) when you have your students do so. Marybeth did not find it to be that simple. Could she relax and focus on her reading? Could she lose herself in a book? It took awhile, but her third-grade students learned not to interrupt her reading during 15 minutes of sustained silent reading.

Renèe, who teaches prekindergarten children, wondered how she could share her adult reading life with those so young. She began simply by letting her students see her reading each day.

Renèe wanted them to realize that she liked to read because she read books that she did not even have to read. She let them see her as someone who reads for pleasure.

Sarah told us about something that happened during DEAR time in her classroom: "I was reading and apparently making some faces because afterward they were asking, 'What happened in your book?'" Michelle's only comment was, "They are watching you," indicating that sometimes the most influential teaching is done through example.

2. Teachers as Readers Talk With Students About Their Reading Lives

Sharon asked her students, "Did I ever tell you about the book that I stayed up all night reading that made me cry?" That kind of question got students' attention. Sharon found that telling about the character Bird in *Before Women Had Wings* by Connie May Fowler (1996) was a powerful way to show that readers can identify with characters and become fascinated with how authors use words.

Sarah let her fifth-grade students know that she was required to read 20 minutes every night and to write about her reading for her university course. She turned in her reading homework to the students so they could question her. This impressed them because they, too, were required to read at home after school each day for 20 minutes. The students loved being able to know their teacher as a reader who thinks about what she reads.

Lori anticipates her annual summer family vacation at the beach. This is a time when she can read whatever books she wants. Even if summer is the only time a teacher gets to live his or her very own reading life, it is still something that can be shared with students. We can come to a new school year ready to tell our students what we have read during the summer and what it has meant to us.

Marybeth surprised her third graders when she began talking about what she was reading after DEAR. She found different ways to share what she was reading. If the content seemed inappropriate for her third graders, Marybeth talked more generally about her emotional responses to the story. After she talked about reading something that made her feel sad, other students began sharing events in stories that made them sad.

Vicki recalled the time she read *The Giving Tree* (Silverstein, 1986) on her last day of teaching fourth-grade students. She knew it was one of those stories she could not read without crying, and sure enough, the students saw her tears as she struggled to read aloud to the end. What mattered to her was that her students understood how the story could initiate such an overwhelming response. Even more remarkable was her understanding that this event totally changed their perspective of her because she had had the courage to show that kind of emotion.

Renèe's prekindergarten students sometimes see her giggling and other times see tears in her eyes while reading. She has decided not to hide from them that reading is an emotional experience for her.

Sarah's students noticed when her eyes filled with tears as she read *Cane River* (Tademy, 2001). Sarah also told her students about getting mad when she read about a sister telling her brother in *Number the Stars* (Lowry, 1998) that he probably could not stay alive without a woman to cook and clean for him.

3. Teachers as Readers Talk About How Their Reading Influences Their Writing

Marybeth read the following excerpt from *Cane River* to teach her third graders that good stories usually have beginnings that grab readers' attention:

> On the morning of her ninth birthday, the day after Madame Francoise Derbanne slapped her, Suzette peed on the rosebushes. Before the plantation bell sounded she had startled awake, tuned her ear to the careless breathing of Mam'zelle above her in the four poster bed, listened for the movement from the rest of the sleeping household, and quietly pushed herself up from her straw pallet on the floor. (p. 3)

"That got their attention," Marybeth told us. Thereafter, children were coming to show her first sentences in their books when they thought them to be good attention-getters, which confirmed that

Marybeth had successfully used a reading example to teach students a point about good writing. She added that sharing from her reading had to be done with "some kind of excitement and enthusiasm." We agreed that if sharing one's reading to teach writing, or anything else for that matter, was done mechanically and without passion, it would lose what the students were responding to.

4. Teachers as Readers Talk About New Vocabulary in Their Reading and How They Go About Understanding It

Pedagogy was Sharon's new vocabulary word. Sharon, who works with elementary school children on their speech and language, began sharing that she, too, came across new words as a reader. Simply sharing that she was a learner about language, just as they were, changed her teaching. Sharon found that the traditional divide between teacher and student became fuzzy when she joined her students as yet another learner.

Another example is the time Barbara talked to her seventh-grade students about reading *Crazy in Alabama* (Childress, 1993). To teach the word *antiseptic*, she read an excerpt about an eye falling out of a socket. Barbara said the boys were particularly interested and wanted to read the book. She refused to give the title because she thought parents might think the book was inappropriate. Imagine the intrigue that Barbara created when she would not reveal the title, and the book was right there in the classroom in a book bag behind her desk.

5. Teachers as Readers Tell Students About the Reader Relationships They Form With Students, Family, and Friends and With Fiction and Nonfiction Characters

Debbie told us about how reading books that her daughter liked had sustained their strained relationship during her daughter's adolescence. We asked her if she had told her seventh-grade students about this. Before being in a conversation about readers as teachers, it had not occurred to Debbie to do so. Possibly the enthusiasm of those in the seminar encouraged her to bring that experience to her teaching by having her students write to family members about the stories they were reading in school.

Tricia wrote about her teacher friend, Carolyn, an avid reader with a home full of books. Tricia trusted Carolyn's reading recommendations, and Carolyn was generous about lending books to her. Tricia's admiration for Carolyn and her love of reading led to the idea of having Tricia's second-grade students interview people from the community about their love of reading. It was this extended relationship between Tricia and Carolyn that gave rise to this educational activity.

Sometimes, Marybeth falls in love with characters in books. She told her third-grade students that she admired Johnnie Mae in *River, Cross My Heart* (Clarke, 1999) because the character fought back when someone insulted her little sister. The students cheered for the character after Marybeth read out loud the paragraph in which the character stands up for herself.

Margret the daughter, the friend, the mother, the wife, and the teacher explored in her essay ways in which reading is inextricably about relationships. She wants reading to be a part of all her family relationships and friendships.

6. Teachers as Readers Tell Students About the Questions They Have While Reading

Jill wondered why she is so interested in reading memoirs and in examining her personal history. She shared that wondering with her university students and read from the author bell hooks about hooks's awareness as a schoolgirl that she was not reading any African American writers. Jill also read from Virginia Woolf, who writes about her realization that there were no books on the history of women on her bookshelf. Reading women's memoirs led Jill to know why she wants to write about her life—her history.

Sarah, who often shared her reader response homework with fifth-grade students, provided them with a model of a reader who questions. On one occasion, she told students about how mad she got while reading Lois Lowry's *Number the Stars* (1998). Sarah wanted to discover how a few sentences about a man needing a woman to cook and clean for him made her so very angry. This type of questioning by readers has been found to be a key dimension of reading comprehension, and one way to teach this skill is by example, which Sarah did by modeling the behavior for her students.

7. Teachers as Readers Tell Students How They Select Something to Read, Why They Sometimes Do Not Finish a Text, and Why They Sometimes Reread a Text

When teachers are readers, they develop their own ways of finding something to read. Jennifer wrote that she sometimes looks through the books in her personal library or goes to the library or bookstore. She, like many of us, also relies on recommendations from people she knows who are reading. Some teachers enjoy rereading favorites, although others do not or do so infrequently. The texts that teachers reread often become more comprehensible and greatly appreciated. For example, Jennifer wrote about realizing that as an adult she understood *Catch-22* (Heller, 1961) in ways that just were not possible when she was an adolescent. Too often, rereading a text is recommended by educators for comprehension solely during the student's initial reading experience, rather than as an important activity the student should continue throughout his or her lifetime. The greater a teacher's awareness of him- or herself as a reader becomes, the more he or she will have to teach students about such realities of being a lifelong active reader.

8. Teachers as Readers Talk to Students About Who Influences Them as Readers—Who Inspires Them

Often we take up a hobby or sport because we know someone who enjoys it. Jennifer remembers having models for reading as a youngster. She recalls titles of books that her sister read and those her parents read. Sharing those memories with students might lead them to notice and comment on readers they know and what they like to read.

Jill wants to encourage her undergraduate university students to take risks as she strives to understand herself as a risky teacher. Sometimes she finds inspiration and support in her reading life. Jill wrote about the words of Helene Cixous that inspire her to continue taking risks.

9. Teachers as Readers Tell Students About Troubles They Have Had With Reading

Perhaps our students are surprised when we let them know that sometimes we think we are reading and then realize we have no clue about what has been happening. When Sarah confessed this to her fifth graders, it led the class to come up with the self-monitoring question, "Huh, what was I reading?"

Margret is a born-again reader. She does not recall finishing one book in high school. Now, she takes a book with her everywhere just in case there is time to read. Margret also remembers as a girl having a special friend who could read better and faster. She did not mind this difference, as long as the friend read to her. These memories converge in Margret the teacher. She relies on her personal history to be a model to her students of the kind of readers she wants them to be, and in doing so, Margret hopes that none of her students will look back on their school years and remember never having finished an entire book.

Someday, Renèe may tell a child how she once struggled with what she thought she should read in order to fit in. Her revelation may reassure the child that everyone has a right to have reading preferences. Readers often have favorite kinds of texts and authors and genres.

10. Teachers as Readers Tell Students About the Strategies They Find Helpful as Readers

Sarah uses sticky notes to mark places in her texts that are important for her to return to. When her students saw this, they began doing it also.

When Sharon told her students about reading *Remembering Blue* (Fowler, 2000), she let them know that in some parts, she slowed down her reading rate so that she could visualize particular scenes. Sharon also told them that in other parts of the book, she read quickly because she was so excited to find out what was going to happen.

11. Teachers as Readers Tell Students About What They Are Learning From Reading

Sarah told her fifth-grade students what she learned from reading the essay *Should We Burn Babar? Essays on Children's Literature and the Power of Stories* (Kohl, 1995). She described her sense of "Aha!" and "Oh, no!" from reading about how famous incidents, such as Rosa Parks's refusal to move to the back of the bus, may have been misrepresented so often that now the myths are better known than the original facts. Students began referring to some authors' writing as "tricky texts." In sharing her reading, Sarah was providing a critical reading lesson that resulted in a term that students understood.

Jill often refers to what she's read to communicate with preservice teachers about what she has learned and is learning about prejudice, racism, white privilege, and issues of power and oppression. Thus, it is through sharing her reading life that Jill shares her values with her students.

12. Teachers as Readers Find Connections Between Their Reading and Their Teaching of Students

Dawn finds in her reading a deeper understanding of the lives of her students. Although she may not have experienced poverty, she can learn what living in poverty means by reading about those who do.

Vicki, who is expected to teach reading according to a particular program, felt guilty whenever she took time at the end of an instructional period to read aloud to first- and second-grade students just for the fun of it. Although Vicki found the mandated reading program beneficial in many ways, she realized that the prohibition against rereading favorite selections was contrary to her own life as a reader. She could not continue to insist that students always bring a new book to read during their sessions. Because of her own joy in rereading, she realized that allowing the rereading of familiar and favorite stories was an important aspect of teaching reading.

Lori felt the character Ellen Foster's words as a wake-up slap in the face. Foster (Gibbons, 1987) could hardly tolerate what she and the other students had to read in school because it was too happy—too perfect—and her life was not that way. Reading that book led Lori to ask herself many questions. She also began asking her elementary school students what they wanted to read, instead of always choosing for them.

Renèe loves to read, but she ran into something unexpected in our Readers as Teachers and Teachers as Readers seminar. Her reading choices seemed far different from the choices of the other teachers. In comparing her reading to that of others, she began feeling inadequate. Fortunately, she talked about this with us and was able to reassure herself that what mattered was the joy she got from reading. Having this experience brought home to Renèe and all of us the possibility that students might end up feeling inadequate among their peers because of what they like to read. The possibility of peer pressure, whether real or imagined, with regard to reading choices was yet another insight gained from Renèe's exploration of her reading life.

Sometimes a character in something we read becomes a touchstone to understanding one of our students. Jill talked about how Lyra in *The Golden Compass* (Pullman, 1996) came to mind when she tried to understand a university teaching intern's fear about doing something different in her mentor teacher's classroom. In the book, Lyra has a spirit guide and sometimes finds herself in conflict between what others expect of her and what her spirit advises. Jill recalled this text because she thought that her teaching intern was experiencing a similar tension between what the mentor teacher expected and what Jill advised.

Aimee grew up loving to read without the extrinsic motivation of earning points. Now she works in a school where children read, take a test, and earn points if they pass. Because Aimee remembers vividly learning to love reading without point motivations, she now strives to get her elementary school students to feel the joy of a good story without any talk of testing and earning points. She knows what that joy feels like, and she will never give up trying to bring that into the lives of her students.

Barbara decided to pass along the thrill she experienced when she could read whatever she wanted for a graduate course. Until the seminar on readers as teachers, it had not occurred to Barbara to grant more reading autonomy to her students. Sometimes, the simplest things elude us until we have direct experience with them. Barbara wanted her students to experience the same sense of pleasure and joy she did when she was given the freedom to read.

13. Teachers as Readers Teach Passionately

During our seminar, there was plenty of passion expressed for being readers and for bringing our reading selves to our teaching of reading. Michelle, Betty B., and Jennifer wondered what would happen to that passion once we were dispersed and back into other school and educational cultures. So we sent the following e-mail to the teachers nine months after the seminar ended when a new school year had just begun:

Dear Readers Who Teach,

Today, we met to move forward on the book manuscript....
We were wondering about something that seems really, really important. We want to know what each of you thinks about the following: What is happening to your being a teacher whose reading life comes into her teaching life, given the current climate of testing, No Child Left Behind, and mandates that affect teaching reading and writing? Are you finding ways to continue being readers who bring your reading lives into your teaching lives? Do you have any advice for teachers who might say, "Hey, bringing my reading life to the teaching of reading doesn't matter because all that matters is children passing tests"? We are hearing stories

about life in schools that seem very discouraging to teachers
who view themselves as professionals and want to make the
important decisions about how best to teach children. Please
reply to the group!

Thanks, Michelle, Betty, and Jennifer

Barbara replied,

I came across a description of what I do to avoid all of the
"junk" in my school, and in education in general in *Phonics
Exposed: Understanding and Resisting Systematic Direct
Intense Phonics Instruction* (Meyer, 2002). It's a description
of the research by Lortie on p. 57. While it probably isn't the
best survival strategy, it certainly works for me, and obviously
others. How sad. I had no idea there were so many others
like me.

Dan Lortie's (1975) research found schools to be cellular,
which resulted in teachers feeling alone. This isolation is why few
teachers talk back to mandates. It feels too risky. Many teachers
make a choice to close their doors and take refuge and safety in
silence. It is poignant to realize that Lortie's research from the
1970s rang so true for Barbara teaching in the new millennium. It
is sad, indeed, to think of how many other teachers might not
realize what Barbara has, that "there were so many others like me."

Sharon replied that the Breakfast Bunche Book Club created
for her third-grade students would be a part of the new school year.
In fact, the media specialist and a lead teacher were launching new
clubs for grades 4 and 5. In regard to her own teaching, Sharon
reported that she had not yet shared much of her reading. She was
feeling torn between presenting students with instruction in
critical areas that they will be tested on and larger issues of
comprehension and expression.

Marybeth reported that the teacher book club she began the
previous winter was growing. At least one new person was going
each month, and several teachers ordered the books that were
being read, even though they could not attend meetings. They
wanted to read the selections anyway. Marybeth was optimistic
because she sensed that the attitudes about testing at her school

were changing for the better. She saw two reasons for this. The first was a new principal who placed less emphasis on testing, and the second was that the results of the previous year's tests were good. Regarding reading in the classroom and sharing books, Marybeth had talked a little about a book she was reading, but she wanted to do more of that.

Annette wrote that she was reading "a lot—for fun, for school, and just because." But she admitted that she had not yet brought her reading life into teaching reading. She was encouraged, though, when she read Sarah's response. We also were excited to hear from Sarah, who was now a second-year teacher of fifth-grade students in a school with 90% free and reduced lunches—a statistic all too often used as a marker for struggling students.

Sarah wrote,

> My advice is that we can never even dream of all of the influence our reading lives have on the children we teach. My students and I wrote letters over the summer, and in every letter I received, students asked me what I was reading and told me that they had been reading, too. This year, I continue to talk about my reading life. Constantly. I still read each night and turn in my homework to my students. I have also joined a few book talk groups that are going on in my classroom. The students keep asking me questions like, "Are you really going to read what we read tonight?" I talk about my reading in minilessons, and we recently had a share day where we all talked about our favorite books. Just yesterday, I brought in an article from *Newsweek* and shared it during our Readers' Workshop. We were talking about reading for different purposes, and I was sharing an article about arthritis that I had read last year as a way of understanding my condition with my knee.
>
> As far as testing is concerned, what can I say? Aren't we leaving children behind if we aren't sharing what readers really do when they read? Sure they must have the skills for the tests, but they also need the skills for life as a reader. I am not sure there is a way to convince teachers that their reading is important. I think we only need to convince teachers to try, just a few times, to bring in their own reading lives, and I don't see how they cannot make time for it.

During one brief semester together, we have remembered and renewed our commitment to be passionate readers who teach. It is still not easy for all of us to stand with our students as engaged and engaging readers, but we each have found more authentic ways to make our reading lives matter in our teaching lives. We challenge ourselves and you, our readers, to find out how these and other stances can enrich any reading program or instructional method.

REFERENCES

International Reading Association. (2000). *Excellent reading teachers*. A position statement of the International Reading Association. Newark, DE: Author.

Kohl, H. (1995). *Should we burn Babar? Essays on children's literature and the power of stories*. New York: New Press.

Lortie, D. (1975). *Schoolteacher: A sociological study*. Chicago: University of Chicago Press.

Meyer, R.J. (2002). *Phonics exposed: Understanding and resisting systematic direct intense phonics instruction*. Mahwah, NJ: Erlbaum.

LITERATURE CITED

Childress, M. (1993). *Crazy in Alabama*. New York: Putnam.

Clarke, B. (1999). *River, cross my heart*. Boston: Little, Brown.

Fowler, C.M. (1996). *Before women had wings*. New York: Putnam.

Fowler, C.M. (2000). *Remembering Blue*. New York: Doubleday.

Gibbons, K. (1987). *Ellen Foster*. Chapel Hill, NC: Algonquin Books.

Heller, J. (1961). *Catch-22*. New York: Simon & Schuster.

Lowry, L. (1998). *Number the stars*. New York: Dell.

Pullman, P. (1996). *The golden compass*. New York: Knopf.

Silverstein, S. (1986). *The giving tree*. New York: HarperCollins.

Tademy, L. (2001). *Cane river*. New York: Warner Books.

Syllabus for READ 9010 (Fall 2001): Readers as Teachers and Teachers as Readers

Michelle Commeyras

This graduate seminar is for those of us who are curious to know more explicitly and specifically how one's personal reading life might be brought to bear on one's teaching life. In the International Reading Association's position statement on excellent reading teachers (2000), there is no mention of the teacher being a reader—having a reading life beyond that of reading to students and being familiar with children's literature. It seems to me that there is much more we can learn about the potential significance of the teacher as reader. I seek to continue my own reading life alongside inservice teachers wanting time to engage in meaningful ways with reading in their everyday lives.

This seminar provides time and space for each participant to set personal reading goals and to select readings to meet those goals. Participants will be engaged in a study of themselves as readers and as readers who teach.

In this inquiry-based seminar, we will pursue the question, What is the potential of a teacher's personal reading for enhancing teaching in general and specifically in teaching reading and language arts?

Our ultimate course goal will be to document what we have learned about being teachers who read and readers who teach.

Proposed Reading and Writing Activities
(Alternative activities ideas are welcome.)

1. Read for your own pleasures, interests, and reasons.

- At minimum, I think we should strive for 30 minutes a day or two and one-half hours a week.

2. Keep a record of your reading life.
   - Choose whatever form fits you. (I keep mine as a file on my computer.)
   - I record full bibliographic information for what I read because I want to read it (for me this includes books, *New Yorker* articles, *New York Times* articles, etc.).
   - I type in regular font with excerpts from the texts that I want to remember or share with you.
   - I type in italics my own thoughts that relate to the content and that relate to our seminar question.
   - I find that keeping this record takes at least 15 minutes a day or one hour and 45 minutes per week.
   - At midsemester, pass in a bibliography of what you have read. You do not need to give me your notes. Your notes will be essential, though, for writing an essay and later a book chapter.

3. Midsemester essay (7–10 typed pages)
   - Write an essay that addresses the seminar question based on what I've learned thus far from my reading life and from our conversations on Tuesday evenings.

4. End-of-semester writing (All together, create a book-length manuscript on Readers as Teachers and Teachers as Readers to submit to International Reading Association for publication!)
   - Revise and further develop my midsemester essay, or
   - Cowrite with one or more persons a chapter-length paper.

Proposed Tuesday Evening Activities (Together, we will think of other things that seem important for us to do together.)

1. While we are arriving and settling in, go to the chalkboard or whiteboard and write down any text titles you want to recommend or comment on and/or write down interesting quotations from your week of personal reading.

2. Have a conversation as a class about what has been written on the board.
3. Have a half hour during which we take turns reading aloud and offering some insights about our lives as readers who teach and teachers who read.
4. Have time near the end of each meeting to write individually or collectively what we are learning that answers our seminar question.

Proposed Course Evaluation

I propose the following chart for the purposes of evaluation.

Reading and Writing Activities	Partially met my/leader's expectations	Met my/leader's expectations	Exceeded my/leader's expectations
Reading daily, weekly, etc.			
Keeping a record of reading life			
Contributing to Tuesday night discussions			
Writing titles and quotations on the chalkboard or whiteboard			
Writing the mid-semester essay on the main question			
Additional activities			